"Artress Bethany White has written a beautiful book that shimmers with bravery on every page. In tackling race, she interrogates and informs, startles and prods, and implicates us all—forcing us to see ourselves through multi-faceted prisms of American identity. Using personal and familial narratives from her own "tangled racial threads" as our intimate guide, White helps us understand this traumatized cultural moment by weaving together harsh truths with poetic language and fierce insight. We need this book right now. White shares an astute pedagogy here, one that acknowledges our collective mourning and provides a prescriptive for our collective healing. I want everyone to read this brilliant collection."
—Bridgett M. Davis, author of *The World According to Fannie Davis: My Mother's Life In The Detroit Numbers*

"*Survivor's Guilt* is an urgent and honest look at one of the most important topics of our time. White is an eloquent storyteller and a deep thinker. She uses her personal life, family history, and teaching experience as a springboard for a wide-ranging discussion of race in America today. These essays are unflinching yet ultimately hopeful. This is one of the wisest books I have read in a long time."
—Sharon Harrigan, author of *Playing With Dynamite*

"In *Survivor's Guilt: Essays on Race and American Identity*, Artress Bethany White offers her personal take on some of the most important issues facing the country today. But rather than tackle political policy or electoral politics, White opens a family album and reflects upon what the nation's failure to reckon with its history has meant for her ancestors' and her past, as well as her own, her husband's, and their children's present and future. If you have been looking for a heartfelt, well-informed, but gentle entry into contemporary thinking about racial concerns—from the legacy of lynching, to the challenges of interracial marriage, to the complexities of class within the black community—you have found your guide."
—Evie Shockley, author of *Semiautomatic*

SURVIVOR'S GUILT

SURVIVOR'S GUILT
ESSAYS ON RACE AND AMERICAN IDENTITY

Artress Bethany White

New Rivers Press is a nonprofit literary press associated with Minnesota
State University Moorhead.

Cover and interior design by Emily Groth
Author photo by Christopher Descano
The publication of *Survivor's Guilt: Essays on Race and American Identity*
is made possible by the generous support of Minnesota State University
Moorhead, the Dawson Family Endowment, and other contributors to New
Rivers Press.

NRP Staff: Nayt Rundquist, Managing Editor; Kevin Carollo, Editor;
Travis Dolence, Director; Trista Conzemius, Art Director
Interns: Gabbie Brandt, Dana Casey, Alex Ferguson, Katie Martinson,
Delaney Noe, Lauren Phillips, Olivia Rockstad

Survivor's Guilt: Essays on Race and American Identity book team: Sarah
Ernster, Alex Ferguson, Aubrey Johnson

∞ Printed in the USA on acid-free, archival-grade paper.

Survivor's Guilt: Essays on Race and American Identity is distributed
nationally by Small Press Distribution.

New Rivers Press
c/o MSUM
1104 7th Ave S
Moorhead, MN 56563
www.newriverspress.com

*For the Bell family, the White family,
the Hairstons, and all American families*

CONTENTS

Introduction

A series of pivotal events led me to write the essays contained in *Survivor's Guilt: Essays on Race and American Identity*. Over the past decade, I have faced the challenge of raising a transracial family in the South, reckoned with being descended from one of the largest slaveholding families in America, and confronted the history of a nineteenth-century ancestor being lynched by the KKK. As I worked to assess these realities, I marveled at how my experiences were echoed in the trauma of a nation under siege from domestic terrorism, gun violence, and racism. In the spirit of healing, I share *Survivor's Guilt* with a public searching for answers to America's complex racial dilemma.

Our nation struggles to process recent acts of national violence, which have become a litany of American tragedy, eliciting plenty of heartbreak but offering few answers: the shooting deaths of nine members of the Mother Emanuel AME Church on June 17, 2015, in Charleston, South Carolina; the Pulse nightclub shooting on December 12, 2016, in Orlando, Florida, which took the lives of forty-nine people; the shooting at an outdoor concert from the Mandalay Bay Hotel, on October 1, 2017, in Las Vegas, Nevada, which took the lives of fifty-eight people; the Marjory Stoneman Douglas High School shooting, on February 14, 2018, in Parkland, Florida, which took the lives of seventeen people; the shooting at the Tree of Life synagogue, in Pittsburgh, Pennsylvania, on October 27, 2018, which took the lives of eleven people; and the shooting at the Walmart in El Paso, Texas, on August 3, 2019, which took the lives of twenty-two people. Additionally, over the past several years, racial profiling has resulted in devastating loss of life: of Trayvon Martin on February 26, 2012, in Sanford, Florida; Tamir Rice on November 22, 2014, in Cleveland, Ohio; Eric Garner on July 17, 2014, in Staten Island, New York; Michael Brown on August 9, 2014, in Ferguson, Missouri; Walter Scott on April 4, 2015, in Charleston, South Carolina; Sandra Bland on July 13, 2015, in Waller County, Texas; and Stephon Clark on March 18, 2018, in Sacramento, CA. This list is by no means complete but used here to represent a disturbing national trend. Even as we engage in collective mourning, a natural desire emerges to prevent future tragedies from occurring. *How can we prevent such occurrences from taking place, and regroup after they do?*

As a career educator, I am often the person friends and family turn to for answers. In fact, I am inevitably asked the question, "Can you suggest books that I can read to help me better understand American race issues?" I understand this need to know; social justice literacy has been my anchor during present and past American social and political uncertainty. Today, in the face of anti-intellectualism seeking to use national crises to foster xenophobia in the United States, it is vital to share and hear each other's stories about racial and cultural bias in America.

In *Survivor's Guilt: Essays on Race and American Identity*, I present a series of personal essays as political commentary on the state of our nation. While the list of names comprising fallen victims continues to grow, I implore readers not to forget the terrorism that once enabled segregation and racial violence at the hands of supremacist groups, and has now reemerged in the guise of racial bias, homophobic politics, and anti-immigration sentiment. *Survivor's Guilt* answers a resounding *yes* to the question: *Could true understanding be only a shared story away?*

Collected here are my personal thoughts and experiences on social trauma, race, class, sexuality, gender, and immigration, intended to spark important discussion on these same topics in our living rooms, on the playground, in classrooms, and in other familial and communal spaces.

"Survivor's Guilt in the Age of Terrorism" engages in a discussion of hate doctrines that breed domestic terrorism amid the backdrop of the Pulse shooting, and my own imminent loss of a family member from cancer in a city under siege. No one thinks about how a walk to the altar will affect the well-being of their families more than interracial couples. What happens when popular culture works hard to get race history right? Using the release of the film *Loving* (2016) as a launch pad, in "American Noir" I discuss the tangled racial threads of my own family, dating back to colonial America and culminating in my interracial marriage, which defies the negative encroachment of this same history. "Kissing Dixie Goodbye" takes a look at how regional politics can often present themselves in covert ways, even amid the most geographically beautiful Southern landscapes. In contrast, "A Lynching in North Carolina" unravels the historical record about lynchings in America and why the legacy has become a popular touchstone in contemporary United States culture.

Desegregation and legislative acts only go so far in preventing racial microaggressions enacted in public spaces. As a result, people of color often have to navigate life through hostile environments while working to escape cultural profiling. In "Pull and Drag," I examine why the racial "talk" is a mainstay in African American life to protect children of color, and to prepare them for a world that is often unwelcoming.

"Childhood Keepsakes" dissolves the line between pedagogy and practice by outing American romanticization of Native American history at the cost of rendering contemporary Indigenous literature invisible.

The need for diverse stories is not a new phenomenon. Multiculturalism hit mainstream education during the 1980s and '90s when the publishing industry began supporting stories written by first- and second-generation immigrants. This interest coincided with increasing numbers of international faculty of color on university campuses. "When I Say Africa, You Say . . ." chronicles my initial exposure to a large African community in New York City, and to literature of the African diaspora, and how I have parlayed this early affiliation into active pedagogy.

Though it is not often addressed, both students and faculty struggle in the contemporary classroom to process the myriad threats that pose challenges outside the hallowed walls of academe. From working through mental illness, losing friends and loved ones to suicide, or trying to resolve trauma through self-medicating, work-life balance often seems like a goal just beyond reach. "I Want to Live, and I Want Everyone Else to Want It, Too" examines the connections between educational initiatives, social distress, and how young adults often react when their world begins to crumble.

In "'Facing It': Of Soldiers, Patriotism, and Literary Resistance," I take a brief look at American patriotism through the lens of two poets writing about the Vietnam War. I call out what we need to remember about war, patriotism, and the myth of American invincibility today.

Gun violence has touched all Americans as a familial or communal narrative. The methodology for telling our stories of personal tragedy can become a cautionary tale while also acknowledging a life cut down too soon. In "Sonny Boy: An Elegy," I peel back the shroud of history on the story of brothers in my own family forced into manhood too soon by World War II, and mortally separated by domestic gun violence.

"Hard-Headed Ike: A Paean to Black Boyhood" examines my early understanding of black masculinity in America through the lens of my own family, while "Burger Princess: On the Business of Being Upper-Middle Class and Black" explores my parents' decision to become Burger King franchisees and prove that the black experience in America was not predicated on an economic pipe dream. Finally, "Be Ready: Tales of Racial Ambushing in the Academy" addresses the struggle to fearlessly tell the true stories of a racially diverse America from the other side of the lectern.

This book rests at the crossroads of memoir and collaborative effort toward community-building. It opens a window into what it means to partake of the history, personal experiences, and literature of those outside our own limited subject position.

1

SURVIVOR'S GUILT IN THE AGE OF TERRORISM

Pulse was not the first act of terrorism to elicit a visceral response from me. After 9/11, like most people, I was riveted to the television trying to understand the enormity of what was taking place, to find out if I had lost friends and, finally, to listen to the stories of those touched deeply and irrevocably by terrorism.

When I heard about the Pulse nightclub shooting in Orlando, Florida, on June 12, 2016, I was working on the final list of required readings for one of my fall college courses. I had just completed Chicano writer Rigoberto González's collection of essays, *Red-Inked Retablos* (2013), and decided to add it to my course list. I felt that willing students would be intrigued by his engaging prose on reconciling his Catholic faith with his sexual orientation, and coming into a love of writing through reading. His personal journey was powerful and spoke of the reward of working toward personal growth embodied in these telling words: "I've come to terms with Catholicism my own way, without feeling like I'm encroaching on a space I don't belong." Then I heard about the Pulse shooting, and suddenly my plan to thwart homophobia through intellectual growth seemed like a drop in the bucket in the face of hatred behind an automatic weapon.

For weeks afterward, America was consumed with stories of survivors working to mend their shattered lives. These stories were followed by photos of the fallen and all they had left behind. Amid national mourning, I sought a sense of hope through a tally of my own attempts to practice empathy in a complex world.

I considered the previous summer when my husband and I visited his family on Cape Cod. While there, a family friend, the primary caretaker for her then eighty-year-old female partner, said she wanted to go out for a night on the town. She asked if I would be willing to attend a popular gay cabaret show with her. I said, "Sure, I'm game." We enjoyed a great night out, but I also recalled being happy to see the uniformed policeman at the front door of the club that night. I was glad someone had put safety first—and that's how I felt: safe. As far as I knew, the cop was the only one in the club with a gun that night, and that's the way it should have been. I was not thinking about an armed gunman with an agenda turning the evening into a horror show.

My family went on to take our summer vacation in Florida over the Fourth of July weekend in 2016, less than a month after the Pulse nightclub shooting. On Friday, July 8th, I visited an aunt at the very same hospital where many of the wounded were taken. As I drove up to the hospital, I saw a display of white crosses representing the slain. I witnessed the memorial with a heavy heart, the event of the shooting still fresh in my thoughts. Yet the crosses also reaffirmed in my mind the utmost urgency to teach compassion for living bodies, instead of saving our contrite memorials for the dead.

As my oldest daughter and I entered the hospital, we were met by a metal detector and several police officers—a post-Pulse safety measure. I opened my purse and stated the purpose of our visit, all the while marveling at how interconnected our lives really are. On that summer afternoon, my Aunt Louise greeted me with a wide smile and expressive eyes, temporarily displacing my meditations on the Pulse shooting. I always enjoyed visiting her. Over the years, I watched her meticulously renovate and expand her Miami, Florida, Mediterranean-styled ranch. The stucco, pastel-colored compound with a terra cotta roof became a testament to her good taste and her gift of hospitality. Now, here she was with stage-four lung cancer welcoming me into her hospital room.

I sat and held her hand, amazed at the paper-thin texture of her skin. Her fingers were long and thin, a characteristic I had noted other members of my family exhibited as they aged. Still, they were lovely to me; these were the same hands that, in a sturdier incarnation, had brushed my hair into ponytails on many a day. For the past several years she had been struggling with Alzheimer's, a disease that makes its sufferers prisoners in their own bodies; like shadowboxing with ghosts, moments of lucidity could be followed by long periods of disorientation. On this day, however, I found my aunt in a loquacious mood, which was closer to the person she'd been before the disease ravaged her storehouse of fond memories.

As we sparked up a conversation in her hospital room, she became insistent that I remember the professional details of her life: the name of the school where she worked for decades and the names of some of her favorite students. In the moment, I was unsure if her insistence was based on her caretaker using this as a mnemonic device or if she was thinking that, without her input, someone might not get the details right for her funeral program. My aunt was a dedicated micromanager of everyone and everything in her orbit. Now, like shards of splintered glass, her world was impossible to put back together again to hold anything of substance.

Prepared, I pulled out a wad of photographs from my shoulder bag and flipped through them slowly to see if any jogged her memory. I started with her siblings, and we celebrated each one that she identified correctly.

In her eighty-seven years, she had certainly led an enviable life full of good friends, family, and fun. She loved a party, just like the revelers at Pulse, but the difference was they had been cut down in their prime and would never enjoy the extended sunset of her long life.

This brief hospital visit would be my last with my aunt. The Pulse crosses were an uneasy foreshadowing of her sudden death three months later.

Vacation and visits over, and making our way back along I-75 later that night, we witnessed a vast halo of flashing blue lights at the entrance ramp to the interstate in midtown Atlanta. As the bright lights of the city's skyline twinkled around us, it appeared as if forty police cars were gathered on the access ramp. Looking on in awe, we recalled from an earlier news report that it was a Black Lives Matter protest in progress in response to the recent shooting deaths of two African American men by police: Philando Castille in Saint Paul, Minnesota, and Alton Sterling in Baton Rouge, Louisiana. My nineteen-year-old daughter, after hearing about protests and terrorism for the last several weeks, softly asked from the backseat of the car if we were going to stop and join the protest. It was almost midnight. I looked back at my two younger stepchildren, one white and the other black, sleeping soundly in the middle of the van and then back into her earnest face. I quickly responded, "Not this time, honey." Through the rearview mirror, I watched the breaking news retreat behind us until the final faint glow of flashing blue receded into black again.

A few days after my return home from Orlando, I took the time to send Rigoberto Gonzaléz a quick email to thank him for writing about his life as an out Latino male, and then continued preparing for the fall semester. I felt, for the moment, in control of my survivor's guilt. I could not change what had taken place at Pulse, but I could stick to my original plan of teaching tolerance by continuing to help my students learn more about a gay sub-culture they knew little about.

Survivor's guilt is usually associated with those who have directly experienced a traumatic event but managed to walk or be carried away with their physical bodies largely intact. Televised media spin has made survivor's guilt a common condition for regular viewers in the era of terrorism. I understand all too well that sympathy for a gunned-down stranger does not necessarily translate into tolerance for the same body alive and in need of civil rights. After all, hadn't I been confronted with this paradox in my pre-Pulse classroom the previous spring semester while teaching queer theory to English majors? On that occasion, I was screening the film *Brokeback Mountain* (2005) in the class as a conversation starter. I believed its Western setting would appeal to the culture of rugged individualism popular in the corner of Appalachia where I taught. I also felt students would relate to the beautiful panoramic views of the Wyoming mountain ranges, which are echoed in the majestic Smokies of eastern Tennessee. Certainly the culture of rural traditionalism would be familiar to my first-generation college students. Finally, the film featured two straight white males in leading roles: in other words, there was some homage paid to heteronormative ideals.

Hyper-attuned to my denominational college surroundings, I held my breath through a few seconds of the initial intimate scene between Ennis del Mar and Jack Twist. I did this after letting students know that I knew many of them had never watched a film about gay culture, and that I wanted them to focus on the rest of the film and not get hung up on one scene.

In class, the students seemed engaged in the film. Emboldened by my initial success, I found out that my strategy misfired for at least one student on my course evaluations, when she made the observation that she was angered by being forced to watch *Brokeback Mountain* at all—a film that clearly disagreed with her religious beliefs. Her statement brought me back to the reality of living in the Bible Belt in the twenty-first century.

Among church cultures exits the concept of hierarchal, salvific elitism that often finds its way into the classrooms of denominational colleges. Gay people are condemned by virtue of their lifestyle. African Americans are condemned for being a reminder of centuries of racial oppression in America, while white women are condemned for not staying in their place. (Of course, white women can easily reinstate themselves by staying in their place.)

Once, a long, long time ago when I was an Alice student in graduate school Wonderland, I penned a dissertation on the transhistorical use of religious rhetoric in African American literature. A consequence of my course of study is that there is very little dogmatic wool that can be pulled over my eyes. I can recognize a religiosity which denies African American equality in a heartbeat. This is the one-time slave-owning religion Frederick Douglass writes about so eloquently in his autobiographical slave narrative, *A Narrative of the Life of Frederick Douglass, an American Slave* (1845). Its contemporary iteration is a loathsome color-blind religion that does not see racial difference. Instead of doing the work to end racial bias, difference is recast as a more dangerous racial indifference. This indifference gives everyone a pass on fighting the injustice of institutionalized racism or reckoning with personal accountability of calling out bigotry among friends and family. Keep in mind, racial color-blindness is a very simple doctrine for churches in the South and the North to perpetuate, largely because congregations are still often segregated along race lines. Color-blindness renders African Americans and other people of color invisible; I don't see your color because I don't see you—at all. This is the traditionalist baggage students bring into the classroom that educators must navigate like landmines on an intellectual battlefield.

The classroom tends to be a microcosm of what is happening outside the campus gates, and there is a lot happening out there. Alas, this is the semester of heated discussions around gendered bathroom legislation in North Carolina, which would require people to use bathrooms based on their biological sex at birth instead of their preferred gender identification. This is also the semester of the passing of a law in Tennessee enabling mental-health professionals to take a pass on caring for members of the LGBTQ community for religious reasons. *Brokeback Mountain*, and the subsequent issues arising from screening it, helped me cover a lot of important cultural terrain. I pointed out to my squirmy students that when they discussed family in their role as future educators, they at least needed to realize that they would have young people in their classrooms who were being raised by same-sex couples or even wrestling with a coming-out narrative of their own.

Waxing nostalgic, I shared with them the story of one of my undergraduate English professors in Massachusetts during the late '80s who was also openly gay and had an affectation for dressing in knickers, button-downs, and bow ties. Beyond his sartorial finesse, I recalled for them his discussion of gay pride and the problem of not being able to marry his long-time lover. His statement left an impression on me; I remember vividly working out his marital dilemma in my class journal, letting him know that I at least thought he should have the right to marry his partner. I reminded my students that it was not until 2015 that the right to a same-sex marriage was guaranteed on a broad national level, much longer than the length of time between me as an undergrad and a professor with tenure. Longer ago than even the Stonewall riot of 1969, the watershed moment that launched the modern-day Gay Liberation Movement. Often students level the accusation against educators that we are trying to remake them into politically-correct creatures. This belief has made me a proponent of replacing the term "politically correct" with synonyms like empathetic, compassionate, and tolerant. Try making the substitution right now as you read this and you will get the point. Imagine these words coming from the lips of a protesting student: "My professors are always trying to get me to be compassionate." Yes, and you were saying?

After the Pulse shooting, I watched mourners gather from all walks of life to honor in public those who had been directly affected by the event. What I still wrestle with is that people don't realize that empathy for those who are different shouldn't just happen after a body has been gunned down and is no longer seen as a political threat. Behind Pulse was a less discernable composite sketch of hate. This picture was not comprised of a single individual, but of hate doctrines perpetuated in mainstream venues and behind closed doors.

~

It is never easy to pick up life where you left off after a catastrophic event. Pulse was not the first act of terrorism to elicit a visceral response from me. After 9/11, like most people, I was riveted to the television trying to understand the enormity of what was taking place, to find out if I had lost friends and, finally, to listen to the stories of those touched deeply and irrevocably by terrorism. My oldest daughter was too young then to watch the churning loop of CNN coverage, so several weeks after the towers were destroyed, a friend—also a young mother— and I decided to take our girls to Six Flags to keep them from peering around doorframes to view the continued coverage.

The amusement park, unfortunately, was more chilling than sitting in front of the television screen listening to reporters trying to make sense out of post-9/11 chaos. The place was like a ghost town; the brightly colored rides were spinning and the carnival music was playing, but the people were eerily absent. Then, out of nowhere, we felt like we were living through the crash and burn of the towers all over again when a lone jetliner flew overhead. We stopped and stared at each other in fear, holding our kids by our sides, our thoughts racing and our feet immobile. Our minds were of one accord: It was just a plane, right? Or was it?

For months after 9/11, I could not walk into a room without doing a quick survey of my surroundings, carrying out a headcount, and taking stock of all available exits. I would profile rooms for abandoned backpacks or other suspicious bags left unattended or even, sometimes, attended. I would startle at loud sounds in closed spaces, becoming too familiar with the rapid heartbeat that accompanies the fear-provoked fight or flight impulse. It took a long time before I was able to channel my memories of 9/11 into active pedagogy in the classroom.

At some point in my teaching experience, I realized that Islamaphobia among my students had been cultivated by their parents' experiences of 9/11. For them, the collective American trauma had been internalized through annual memorials that often focused on loss. As a result, eight years after the fall of the towers, I decided to teach a class on Muslim women's literature.

Many of my teaching adventures begin as I stand in front of my bookshelves. Over the course of my educational background, both formal and informal, I collected books that served to educate me about women living under Islamic law in one way or another. I read Egyptian feminist critic and author Nawal El Saadawi in the years between my undergraduate and first graduate degree. During my years working on my master's degree, I became acquainted with Senegalese author Mariama Ba, and during my postgraduate years, I became a fan of Somali author Ayaan Hirsi Ali and Syrian-American novelist Mohja Kahf. *The Girl in the*

Tangerine Scarf (2006), a coming-of-age tale of a young girl growing up Muslim in the Midwest during the '70s and '80s, touched me immensely and motivated me to teach the course and invite the author to campus.

Kahf has an open and engaging personality, a quality which made her stand out as a campus visitor as she sported a fashionable headscarf. For the duration of her stay, we became friends, and I became convinced once again that anyone is capable of creating community despite racial and religious differences. This is true, however, only if we remember that the savor of empathy is the sweetest of freedoms.

The most meaningful result of Kahf's visit for students was their realization that cultural difference could lead to an engaged sharing of views not rooted in conflict. They laughed when Kahf read from her fiction and poetry. They nodded sagely when she read from her criticism. They even expressed genuine interest in her discussion of her faith and how it intersected with her life as a writer.

At the conclusion of her visit, I did not ask if my students now felt that they could think about 9/11 and Muslims in a different light. My measure of success was a little different. The point was that the next time someone said *Muslim* or they saw a woman in a headscarf, they might think about an energetic writer who'd had a lot to say, that they were glad they had taken the time to hear. I also hoped they had come to realize a survivor's tale did not have to end with the guilt and fear of the grief-stricken.

2

AMERICAN NOIR

This was the explanation for her fair skin and freckles: determined Scottish genes on an otherwise African tapestry.

It is winter 2016 and my husband and I take a selfie in front of the marquee poster for the film *Loving*. While smiling for the camera, I recall the number of times I have talked about the landmark Supreme Court case in my college classroom as an example of modern American race history; this case, *Loving v. Virginia*, wiped anti-miscegenation laws off the books in 1967. Our heads tilt toward each other to fill the frame, and I marvel at the fact that I married this man now standing beside me in 2012 while living in the South. I did not marry him because of his race; I married him despite it. When I looked into his face, I did not see the detestable history of racial conflict rearing up before me.

Instead, I listened to him talk about a childhood that mirrored my own in more ways than it differed. I, too, gauged my childhood days by family road trips in a paneled station wagon, enjoyed time when parents were away and a maiden aunt stepped into the domestic picture as babysitter, and could relate to his stories of winter snows and spring thaws. My husband was raised in Pennsylvania, while I was raised in Massachusetts. His ancestors hailed from England and my own from Africa and Scotland. In Tennessee, we'd found each other as lost "Yankees" in a Southern stew and grasped onto each other for dear life.

I find that I pay more attention to racially diverse families in the South than I ever did in the North. This is probably because I fear for their safety more in the South. The South still visibly and unashamedly displays its nineteenth-century politics with the stone monuments to the Confederacy and the Confederate flags flying on 100-foot flagpoles along the interstate, as if the Union had been defeated after all. Additionally, there is the tradition of a yelled racial epithet when you least expect it, the segregated churches, and the values of a fallen Southern plantation aristocracy. I still harbor a fear that one day the last vestiges of faux Southern civility will crack irreparably and the newly released rage will be directed at those who have embraced difference the most: the interracial, biracial, and multiracial families.

Under the yoke of Southern traditionalism, avoiding the pitfalls of committing racial microaggressions requires a high level of vigilance, and plenty of people fall asleep behind the wheel. Once after getting a haircut, a young white stylist rang up my bill and then asked me if I wanted to pay for my daughter at the same time. I was immediately taken aback because I'd come into the salon alone. Intrigued, I followed her magenta-tipped finger pointing to an approximately ten-year-old biracial girl getting her long curly hair trimmed. I remembered seeing the girl when I first walked into the salon. Her mother, a white woman, had smiled at me as I entered the door. When I took in her daughter sitting next to her and the curly-kinky quality of her hair, I assumed it was a smile of racial solidarity. I returned the smile. Now, looking back at the stylist after her question, I replied that I would just be paying for my own hair. I did not elaborate, but left it to her to figure out that, yes, the young girl and I were the only blacks in the shop, but, no, she was not my daughter. I could not, however, bear to look into the face of the girl's mother as she sat a mere two feet away. I imagined I would feel hurt in the same situation. I was not interested in intercepting her look of disappointment.

~

I occasionally meditate on the various signs people once looked for to determine race and ancestry: visible half-moons on a black person's nail beds as an indication of white ancestry, the telltale wave in the hair that might denote black ancestry, the milky tan skin tone alerting an observer to look a little more closely at the face in question. People still like to know the racial and ethnic background of those around them so that they can categorize them accordingly. As a result, today it is imperative that white parents who are the caretakers of black children be as prepared as black parents for what it means to enter black world—whether the child came to them through adoption or an interracial relationship. They need to know why, if their child is biracial, they cannot change the world with the stroke of a pen and check "white" in the box designating race on the school personal data form. In America, you cannot be white today and black tomorrow unless, as Louisianans say, you are truly *passé blanc*—one who can unquestioningly pass for white.

When I first started teaching about the "one-drop rule"—the ideology that one drop of black blood could make an otherwise white person black—as a mainstay of the social construction of race in America, I saw the same morbid curiosity reflected in my students' faces that the topic once held for me. This was a world where the black race was recalibrated by sanguine percentages into mulattos, quadroons, and octoroons. History is full of tales of mixed blood and plantation sexual exploitation. Yet, as the acceptability of con-

sensual interracial relationships has increased nationally over the years, I notice that my white and black
Southern students are less reticent about weighing in
on interracial relationships in their own families. In fact,
they often point out these family members as examples of racial progress, even while admitting that their
interracial unions are not always accepted by extended
family members. Still, in some semesters, almost half of
my students have admitted to having a black, white, or
brown relative on a branch of their current family tree.
My own family history makes it easy to identify with
their experience.

As a kid, I recall my father's emphatic words, "Your
mother is not white," after almost hitting the brakes in
the middle of the highway following my offhand reference to my mother's race. Offering proof, he explained
that both of my maternal grandparents were black, which
made her also black, despite her red hair and freckles
which seemed to state otherwise. Corrected, I stared out
the window of the moving car, marveling that I had spent
nearly the first decade of my life believing my mother
was white because of her fair skin, hair that did not kink,
a face full of lentigines, and feet that were the same color
on top as they were on the bottom.

Realistically, I should not have been blamed for mis-
reading my gene pool as a kid. After all, my parents had
separated during my infancy, and my father had always
been my custodial parent; I could count on one hand the

number of times I'd visited my birth mother before graduating high school. Still, I had accepted, in my child's mind, that my mother was white, and it certainly didn't change the fact that she was my mother—despite my own deeper, brown complexion. I guess you could say I forgave her for not looking more like me, which meant I forgave her for her skin color—the exact shade of dry sand on an expanse of sun-kissed beach. Color was the obvious difference between this mother and daughter, but while gazing into my bathroom mirror one day, I'd spied a distinctive sprinkle of freckles across my nose. This single shared trait kept everything blood-simple.

To explain my maternal line of tangled blood ties, my mother passed along her knowledge of a Scottish ancestor named Peter Hairston and a rough date of his landing in British America in the early 1700s. She explained that members of our family were enslaved by the Hairstons and, over time, became related to them. During this conversation, she also told me about my great-grandfather and the significance of his middle name: Gilchrist. According to my mother, the name had been passed down in her family for generations. To maintain the tradition, she ensured that my younger brother would also bear the middle name Gilchrist for a new generation.

Learning about my interracial ancestry in North Carolina as a child was a novel experience and gave me a different vision of my heritage beyond the bowels of a slave ship. Yes, my African ancestors experienced the Middle Passage and proved their resilience by living to see a distant, American shore, but they had also become a part of the American dream of an immigrant from Scotland. The two lines, black and white, built an enduring plantation empire spanning Virginia, North Carolina, and Mississippi. I could claim the name, the history, and the blood, sweat, and tears of both sides. This oral slave narrative was the explanation for her fair skin and freckles: determined Scottish genes on an otherwise African tapestry. My family history was truly the stuff of a mixed-blood American reality.

I would later learn that a white member of the Hairston family fought for the Confederacy during the Civil War. This is not surprising, considering that a single member of the same family had once owned several thousand slaves, and the calculated holdings of the entire family over the course of institutional slavery in the U.S. was, by one estimate, 10,000 slaves. In a 1989 *New York Times* article, I read the story of how the Hairston family reunion, founded by my black great-grandfather William G. Hairston, became a modern-day white and black affair, seeking to erase the barriers erected by that same Civil War. While white family descendants may still reside on plantation lands, there is also a black family parallel history. This history is recalled in the pride I felt after visiting the one-room Pine Hall Colored School (now a deteriorating local historic landmark) on a North Carolina mountaintop. Here my maternal great-grandfather, William G., instructed his classes in the early twentieth century and, in the same region, left many acres of land to his own eight black children.

In his book *The Cooleemee Plantation and Its People*, the namesake and great-grandson of Civil War-era Peter Hairston includes an index listing the names and birthdates of the enslaved from his branch of the Hairston family. The names of many of my ancestors are on this list. Using the details from the oral slave narrative I inherited from my mother, the Cooleemee Plantation records, and vital statistic records, I was able to put together a narrative of my great-grandfather's birth, marriage, and creation of a family of his own.

Born on a plantation in 1865, evidence supports William G. being conceived by his enslaved mother Mima, who was still listed as Peter Hairston's plantation property for that year, and her master. Additionally, her newly born son, Gilchrist (also spelled Gillcriss), was listed as her progeny with an 1865 birthdate in the same documentation. The name Gilchrist resonated strongly for me as I looked through these slave records, because part of the oral slave narrative that was passed down to me by my mother centered on the importance of William G.'s middle name, not his first name. This significant middle name is how he is listed on plantation records connecting him to his mother, Mima. Later I would find other public records that tied mother and son together by name. These records would include

William G.'s 1891 marriage license documenting the beginning of his family life with my great-grandmother, Sallie Fulton. On this document, he lists Mima as his mother and Peter Hairston as his father.

Another aspect of my mother's oral slave narrative claimed that my great-grandfather was a blood descendant of the original Peter Hairston who immigrated from Scotland and his subsequent descendants. On a post-Emancipation census, Mima is listed as "mulatto." It would stand to reason that she also was a descendant of white Hairstons. If, indeed, his master was his father, this made William G. a "quadroon" in the racial parlance of slavery, meaning that he was only one quarter African American. William G. was conceived on the eve of slavery's demise in the South. His mother Mima was a fourteen-year-old slave girl in 1864 when she realized that she would become a mother. Her life, like the lives of many of the enslaved, had not yet changed despite Abraham Lincoln's 1863 Emancipation Proclamation, which legislatively ended the institution of slavery. This legislation, however, did not guarantee that every slave was in a position to or allowed to walk away from enslavement without the direct support of the Union Army.

Upon closer investigation of the Peter Hariston slave roster, I noted that Mima was born in 1850. She was one of seven children attributed to Eady in the Civil War-era Peter Hairston slave ledger: Mint, Diannah, Dotts, Suck,

Ruth, Roseanne, and Mima. All of them were listed in Peter Hairston's mid-century estate holdings, which included the Cooleemee Plantation—now a North Carolina historical site. I then recalled that I had encountered Eady's name previously in the 1870 census record where her name was also listed as Edith. While this was a horribly casual way to find out the name of my great, great, great-grandmother, it was still a watershed moment. Suddenly I realized that my mother's oft-told story of our family slave legacy had initiated my journey toward finding out the names of the ancestral matriarchs in my family.

One of the reasons my mother was so frustrated in her later years about our family history was that a book written about the Hairston family in 1999 failed to mention her grandfather, William G. Hairston, at all. She couldn't believe that a Hairston who had been so influential in his community had been left out of history during family interviews that had taken place in North Carolina. She even questioned the author about the omission at one of the Hairston family reunions. The author, however, did not have the oral slave narrative at his disposal when he wrote the book and perused the historical record; I, however, did. What at one time seemed like a few historical details repeated verbally over generations made all the difference in me being able to chart my great-grandfather's genealogical line among a lengthy listing of the names of the enslaved.

While Henry Wiencek's *The Hairstons: An American Family in Black and White* (1999) failed to mention William G. Hairston at all, he may actually have included earlier iterations of William G.'s family tree. Evidence reveals that the black Hairstons in my line made a point of recycling names to indicate genealogy. Going back twenty-four years before my great, great, great, grandmother Eady's birth in 1821, another Mima appears in a family tree contained in his book as a daughter of Robert Hairston and his slave mistress, Sally Blag. In fact, one of this first Mima's siblings was also named Gilchrist.

Transgenerational naming practices, in this case, indicated the intentionality of enslaved people to accurately represent their blood ties to their European enslavers. It also presents a strong possibility that this earlier Mima was somehow connected to Eady. Wedding context to content, I realized that I might actually have traced my maternal bloodline back seven generations from my birth to my great, great, great, great, great-grandmother Sally Blag's birth on United States soil in 1770.

The sexual practices of planters in regard to their slaves often involved convoluted, hypocritical, and unethical acts. What happened to enslaved females in particular was based on the added economic value of children born into slavery. Sexual exploitation between enslaver and female slaves became acceptable practice because slaves were considered property instead of fully-realized men and women. Additionally, there were often attempts made to hide these relationships in family records. It is not beyond the scope of reason that slaves reused names as a way of indicating red flags in their own communities that would help other slaves choose their domestic partners more carefully in order to protect their gene pool.

William G., however, survived and thrived despite his plantation birth to become the epitome of promise embodied in a postbellum free black man; he came of age as a literate farmer and landowner. According to my mother, William G. was an imposing figure—a tall fair-skinned man with bright blue eyes and blond hair that turned to snowy white in his later years. Though he earned no doctorate, once he became a rural schoolteacher he was called "Professor" throughout his lifetime by his African American students. To ensure knowledge of the black Hairston lineage and William G.'s accomplishments for the next generation, my mother passed on his distinctive middle name to my brother, William G.'s great-grandson—a name to bind both history and memory.

Linking memory and American history through the black body is often denied in American dominant culture. A case in point is the number of years it took scholars like Annette Gordon-Reed to prove that the relationship between Thomas Jefferson and his slave, Sally Hemings, had brought forth children with direct genetic lineage to the third U.S. President. I never questioned the story that my mother told of our heritage, because, in part, the truth of it was inscribed on her body. Later I would discover that our slave history was documented in both archival records and in publication, but it was still a natural progression to investigate what a DNA test would say about my ancestry. The results indeed revealed that almost thirty percent of my DNA was European, with twenty-five percent of it coming directly from the British Isles with a Scottish marker. While my ancestry was hidden under skin that would never define me as anything other than African American, this was not the case for my mother and many of William G.'s other descendants.

Typical of black people hailing from the same family, William G.'s children came in more than one shade. When I met Annie, the oldest of his daughters, I marveled at her light brown skin, so much closer to my complexion than my mother's. I gained a different perspective when, as a child, I met his second oldest daughter, Ida. She was a white-appearing black woman with gray hair who fed me cinnamon red hearts from the kitchen cabinet as a treat during my brief visit to her spacious home. Her husband, Uncle Clarence, was a cheerful, dark-skinned black man who, on this occasion, gave me and my cousins enough money to go to the now defunct Rocky Point Amusement Park in nearby Warwick, Rhode Island. Their old Victorian home also captivated my attention. I remember how impressed I was to be in a house with a front and rear staircase and circular turret rooms with dumbwaiters. I must have left an impression on her as well; while my Aunt Ida, who was actually my great aunt, never had children of her own, she managed to leave almost all of her northern relatives a token monetary inheritance. Her small gift came in handy for much-needed meal and entertainment funds while I was an undergraduate at the University of Massachusetts, Amherst.

William G.'s daughter Ida Bynum, nee Hairston, was the first to migrate to Providence, Rhode Island, from North Carolina with her husband, Clarence. She established herself by purchasing that Victorian house on the east side of the city in 1944, and later took in black boarders as a steady source of income. She was among the second generation of free blacks after Southern emancipation, and her economic industry was tremendous. She paved the way for other members of her family to migrate north. Her home became an anchor and weigh station of possibility. She was soon joined by her sister Mary, my maternal grandmother, and her family comprised of a husband with North Carolina roots, two daughters, and a son. After some time in the North, the Ellingtons went on to secure their home and economic stability. Mary became a schoolteacher, while her husband, James, worked as a groundskeeper for nearby Brown University. Providence was my mother's childhood home until she met and married my father while completing her nursing degree.

Over the years, my mother had given me glimpses into her childhood and adulthood when, not surrounded by darker-skinned members of her family, she was not immediately identifiable as African American. This was confirmed by my father when he confessed that the first time he brought her to the small Southern town of his birth, many of his friends at first glance believed he had married a white woman during a time when it was still remarkable to do so. I think I understood my mother's journey best, though, when we visited her grandfather's ancestral home near her birthplace of Winston-Salem, North Carolina.

Here in the towns of Pine Hall and Walnut Cove, time seemed to stand still. While these hamlets had also been touched by the modern-day ravages of the outside world, including opioid and meth addiction visited upon their remaining young people, they simultaneously retained an air of the lived rhythms of a bygone era. Here, I saw face after face inscribed with the history of slavery, and understood that this was a place where my mother did not have to explain her coloring or her blackness: in this place, everyone knew what the DNA of slave history meant.

The play of light and dark has continued on my mother's side of the family in later generations, though the politics of these relationships are much different. Interracial marriages have produced nieces who confront the same questions about their fair skin and racial identity that my great-grandfather, mother, and great aunt faced during the racially charged eras of Southern Reconstruction, Jim Crow, and American Civil Rights. Today, their personal journeys of racial reconciliation are nothing unusual within a nation still struggling with its own diversity and racial complexity.

For the uninitiated, navigating American race politics is a challenge that seems like it should come with its own how-to manual. I like to imagine a racial tool kit being comprised of historical data. Picture a large old leather trunk with an ornate hasp and a key that magically materializes in your palm when you need it most. In it are all the published records to explain the micro and macro racial aggressions one might encounter in a given day. It might include a reading list of books beginning with the tales of doomed fictional, mixed-raced heroines of the nineteenth century (commonly known by the denigrating genre title "tragic mulatto tales") who could not find a stable home in the black or white world, and had to be killed off or relegated to a nun's life to prevent them from introducing their "one drop" of black blood into future generations of unsuspecting white families. These fictions once provided a historical context for prescriptive American race relations. The rules were clear and could be summed up thusly: do not engage in melting-pot sexual relations despite the democratic idealism on which the nation was founded.

The history of race relations in America is long and winding, and without the historical context, it is impossible to master its intricacies, resulting in plenty of casualties.

It is the twenty-first century, but biracial young people must still face the awkward question of "What are you?", or engage in the process of adult acculturation into the black world necessary after growing up in predominantly white communities and schools. Additionally, a negation of default white beauty standards is still something that has to be taught by parents. Even black parents of black children must do this work, because the constant barrage of what constitutes beauty in the film and television industry is dependent on European aesthetics. The tragedy is not biraciality, but children who feel that they must suffer through ignorance and taunting because they do not know the survival stories of those who came before them. It is terrible to believe oneself a pioneer instead of part of a centuries-old genealogical and literary tradition. To counter this dearth of information, also in the trunk one should find a stack of newer mixed-race narratives that bring the discourse current. These volumes might include the "tween" novel *Blended* (2019) by Sharon M. Draper, poet Natasha Trethewey's *Native Guard* (2006), James McBride's memoir *The Color of Water: A Black Man's Tribute to His White Mother* (1995), Heidi Durrow's novel *The Girl Who Fell From the Sky* (2010), and Danzy Senna's *Where Did You Sleep*

Last Night? A Personal History (2009).

Today, my own nuclear family is a web of mixed blood and history, comprised of one biracial daughter, one black daughter, and two white sons. Our racial tool kit is a well-stocked library and does not dwell in a trunk at all. We annihilate the myth that books about the true racial experience in America have never been written whenever we head to the bookshelves to negotiate the complex race history that has birthed us all.

3

KISSING DIXIE GOODBYE

We understood collectively that bigotry is catching; like a flu, it will get to you eventually, no matter how frequently you wash your hands among the contagious.

I fell in love with the Shenandoah Valley the first time I saw it. The sun shone brightly through intermittent clouds floating overhead and created the illusion of folds along the verdant green mountain range. As a kid traveling south with my family, I promised myself I would live there one day. Though the valley below was only dotted with farms and fields of cattle, and I had no aspirations to own either a farm or livestock, the mountain range won my heart. Years later, I recalled those thoughts while travelling up through the Shenandoah Valley with two of my stepchildren in tow. Every now and then I would yell toward the back seat, "Kids, come on, look at that

majestic view." They in turn sighed heavily, ungluing
their faces from their respective iPads with a dismissive,
"Yeah, nice," before diving right back into cyberworld.
The beauty was lost on them, but it didn't stop me from
interrupting a few more times just so I wouldn't feel
guilty for not trying. In the summer of 2017, driving
through the Shenandoah Valley represented something
else for me: this was my proof that I was finally returning to the North after too many years away. What I didn't
know when I was a child was that geography, as beautiful as it is, often harbors politics that are not culturally
inclusive, and are too often blatantly dangerous.

I remind myself regularly that I should not idealize
my return to the North, because to do so would be a
setup for disappointment. After all, I was returning to
live in Pennsylvania, the very state that had gone from
blue to red in the 2016 presidential election. Add to that
the realities of racism I have faced in the North and the
South, and the truth is evident that racism is a pandemic
knowing no regional borders. Still, it was reassuring
this past winter to see one of those post-election signs
planted in a snowy yard while house hunting with my
husband before our move to Philadelphia. You know, the
signs that state: "In Our Community, Black Lives Matter,
We Fear No Faith, Women's Rights are Human Rights,
No Human is Illegal, Science is Real, Love is Love."
As I read this one I thought, *I am surely in the
right place.* Here was a self-identified human being

claiming a sanctuary for all of us who desired to live in a compassionate world. *Hugs and kisses to you, too, my new Philadelphia neighbor*, I thought.

Imagine my delight when, a scant few months later, our eight-year-old brought home her three new girlfriends during the first week in our Pennsylvania neighborhood: a Haitian-American, an English-Chilean American, and an Asian-American. The great melting pot of America I had previously experienced living in Boston and New York was now replicated in Philadelphia. Our next-door neighbors were even an interracial couple.

My social groups while living in Tennessee were largely politically segregated. People often cultivate homogeneous communities in places where diversity is considered a dirty word. I spent a lot of time around other African Americans, self-identified liberal whites, and people of color—all those who at least attempted to empathize with or understand my subject position. Within this group, I found other educators, writers, and artists joined in solidarity to make inroads into outdated Southern cultural politics. Each couple had their own reasons for desiring change. Some were parents resulting from transracial adoptions, and others were in interracial or transcultural marriages. Many just wanted, at the very least, to create a better, more inclusive world for their own children; they approached the task with a sure knowledge that if they did not work hard, their own visibly white children would absorb the racist rhetoric they heard around them on school playgrounds and someday verbally oppress the children of their multiracial friends. You bet they felt a burning need to share their pedagogies for change with others who would actually employ them. We understood collectively that bigotry is catching; like a flu, it would get to you eventually, no matter how frequently you washed your hands among the contagious.

It was only a week after the 2016 presidential election when my husband came into the house looking wild-eyed and excited, claiming, "You won't believe what just happened to me at the supermarket." Catching his breath, he told me that he'd just prevented a fight from breaking out in the fruit and vegetable section of our local supermarket. Apparently, a six-foot-five male had verbally attacked another gentleman a foot shorter than himself. The shorter man was brown-skinned, but my husband couldn't specify his race. Not realizing that he was being watched intently, the brown-skinned man taste-tested a grape before deciding whether or not to purchase a bag of them. After popping the fruit in his mouth, the tall guy, who was white, said "Do you plan on buying those or what?" Surprised, the shorter man turned toward his accuser with a muttered "Wh—at, I…" Not waiting for the guy to piece a sensible response together, the big guy took another step closer to the grape-eater and said, "Why don't you just go back to your own country." This is when my husband, who is six-foot-four, stepped between the two and said,

"Hey, why don't you just leave him alone? He isn't bothering you." Surprised that another white man would question his right to accost a man who appeared to be an immigrant, Tall Guy turned on my husband and asked, "Why? Is he a friend of yours or something?" At this point, losing his taste for the battle, the man muttered a few words under his breath and went back to his own shopping. My husband admitted that the whole incident rattled him. We both wondered how our lives might change in the South after the election, and suddenly this incident gave us an indication.

Philadelphia is at the tail-end of Appalachia, so far from the center that people pronounce the word *Appalay-sha* instead of *Appa-latch-a*. The major difference I notice when I arrive in the Northeast again is that more people look me in the eye instead of at my cheek or just to the left or right of my head when addressing me. I learned in the South that people try to avoid eye contact if they habitually talk about their dislike of blacks within their regular milieu. They believe that if they look you in the eye, you will suddenly be privy to the number of times they have used the n-word in the past month or the number of times they have accessed websites that endorse putting an end to at least three things in America: immigration, interracial marriage leading to the "mongrelization" of society, and black leadership.

I first experienced this unfocused look during my time as a graduate teaching assistant in Kentucky when I was working on my doctorate. I was helping a student who volunteered that he had been home-schooled and had not read the typical books considered part of the expanded Western canon during his high school studies. After running through some typical titles including *Lord of the Flies*, *The Scarlet Letter*, and *The House on Mango Street*, I asked if he had ever read a novel at all. After a long pause, he admitted to reading *The Swiss Family Robinson*. Keep in mind that all of this was said as he swung his gaze between my chin and cheek. I marveled again at the number of people who home-schooled their children in the South so that they could teach creationism versus evolution, opt out of race and LGBTQ studies, immigration discourse, colonialism, and feminism. The first two weeks of my course based on culturally diverse literature so alarmed this young man that he ended up dropping the class. This clearly did not represent the demographics of his rural Kentucky town of approximately 7,300.

~

Sadly, not too many weeks after my move to Philadelphia, Bianca Roberson was shot in the head on a Pennsylvania highway. This tragedy was overwhelming for me. My thoughts were haunted by the idea that an eighteen-year-old black girl, on the eve of what would have been her freshman year in college, was profiled. Her murder at the hands of a white male driver was supposed to be a case of road rage, but who can say whether she was provoked into a cat-and-mouse game on a highway that was not of her own choosing. In the political climate of Trump's America, how were local citizens supposed to accept the extreme behavior of a young white male using a handgun on a black woman driving away from his vehicle? The level of silence from others around me after this event spoke to a fear that people could not voice: if this was a new method of hate crime enactment, by not calling it out, hopefully it would quickly fall from favor. This belief, in my mind, was as horrifying as the crime itself. From a regional perspective, Bianca Roberson's murder proved there was nowhere to run or hide.

Of course, hiding is never really an option for politically-conscious people of color in America. After another recent college football game, where a player was reprimanded after kneeling during the anthem in protest of police violence against members of the African American community, I reached for my copy of Ta-Nehisi Coates' *Between the World and Me* (2015). I did so because I was awed by the habit of some academics, including those on this northern college campus, to still address the kneeling issue as if it was about the American flag and the national anthem. To be clear, there is not a problem with the anthem and the flag when both continue to symbolize a nation that respects the rights of all people. When, however, institutions within that same nation systemically and violently disenfranchise a large segment of a population based on race, protest is the logical way of getting said institutions to reexamine themselves. Too many black bodies are still denied the agency to live life itself. Coates' book-length letter to his son reminds us of this in the following excerpt:

> *I write you in your 15th year. I am writing you because this was the year you saw Eric Garner choked to death for selling cigarettes; because you know now that Renisha McBride was shot for seeking help, that John Crawford was shot down for browsing in a department store. And you have seen men in uniform drive by and murder Tamir Rice, a 12-year-old child whom they were oathbound to protect. And you have seen men in the same uniforms pummel Marlene Pinnock, someone's grandmother, on the side of the road. And you know now, if you did not before, that the police departments of your country have been endowed with the authority to destroy your body. It does not matter if the destruction is the result of an unfortunate overreaction. It does not matter if it originates in a misunderstanding. It does not matter if the destruction springs from a foolish policy. Sell cigarettes without the proper authority and your body can be destroyed. Resent the people trying to entrap your body and it can be destroyed. Turn into a dark stairwell and*

your body can be destroyed. The destroyers will rarely be held accountable. Mostly they will receive pensions. And destruction is merely the superlative form of a dominion whose prerogatives include friskings, detainings, beatings, and humiliations. All of this is common to black people. And all of this is old for black people. No one is held responsible.

It is a dire lament when a parent has to put into words what their child sees: people who look like me are killed, and their killers can still walk away without doing time for the crime. Likewise, when a black athlete exercises agency over his own body, a body that a largely white industry benefits from, that agency will be challenged again and again, and defined as a crime unto itself.

Coates and other writers exploring race in America remind us that anyone who wants to walk with confidence in a multiracial world must read broadly. Cross-cultural understanding can lead to friendships that are more enduring when they begin on the same page. Further, multicultural literacy helps in avoiding those errors that will ensure a friendship is short-lived. I am talking real friendships here—not the relationship you might have with the postal person who may deliver your mail, or the soccer mom or dad you chat with while your kids engage on the field; that is basic human civility, not friendship. That single woman or man will never succeed in being the storehouse of information for what

you need to know about people of color in America.
Cultural curiosity should be both intimate and broad
and should involve reading, travel, and the partaking of
cultural arts.

Beyond friendship, cross-cultural immersion through
literature is also a way to stem the tide of domestic
hate crimes at the micro and macro level. My belief is
affirmed when I am reminded of a 2017 incident covered in the *New York Times* that detailed Judge Avelina
Jacob's ruling that a group of young people who defaced
a historic African American schoolhouse in Ashburn,
Virginia, be sentenced to reading about diverse cultures
as punishment. The irony here, which the judge realized
as well, is that this was not punishment at all, but a gift.
She bequeathed them with the eradication of ignorance
and an opportunity to reexamine their own humanity—which they had clearly lost sight of. Some of the
proposed books on the list included predictable choices
that currently reside on many mainstream middle school
reading lists, like Elie Wiesel's *Night*. According to the
reporting on the case, some of these students claimed
to not even know what a swastika symbolized but still
spray-painted it on the historic site's walls. With this
assertion in mind, Wiesel's book is a rich storehouse of
information on the Holocaust, which would then allow
teachers to show pictures of Nazi use of the symbol
in its proper context. Despite what many intellectuals
living in major cities might think, however, often in

rural school districts, Wiesel's book doesn't even make it across a high school student's desk. I myself have faced Holocaust deniers in Southern college classrooms. In my experience as a post-secondary educator at both research institutions and small liberal arts colleges, the only students who regularly read contemporary novels and nonfiction based on culturally diverse communities are enrolled in honors or advanced placement classes. This is just another means by which essential education becomes elitist.

I have spent plenty of time teaching in rural and urban communities. The way I work to improve generational retention of diverse narratives is to advise my students, regardless of their major, to purchase the books for my classes instead of renting them to save a few dollars, something that is not easy to convince underfunded college students to do. I encourage them to build personal libraries that they can share with their family members and, one day, maybe even their children. As first-generation college students, I tell them not to hesitate to share the books with their mothers and fathers. More than once, students have come back to tell me how much a parent has enjoyed a novel. The simple truth is that good stories change lives.

Despite my own inroads into student racial bias, I often find my white educator colleagues, both in the South and in the North, are unwilling to address race in their own classrooms because it makes them uncomfortable. Yet there is no reason for this. The easy solution is they must deflect from themselves as experts and, instead, defer to others who have written extensively on the topics they most want to address. There are plenty of authors writing from the trenches of race activism at this particular moment in history. Too often we forget that intellectual development does not end with the receipt of a terminal degree, and is deepened by life-long reading both inside and outside of our fields of specialization. Empathy begins with working to understand the very communities we neglect. It is amazing to think about what real change would look like on the cultural landscape if more educators took up the challenge.

~

Now, when I travel back to Tennessee as a visitor, what I notice is that Southern traditionalism has many guises, and it is often hidden in plain sight. It reared into my sightline again on a recent trip to Dollywood with my family. This was not my first trip to the theme park, viewed as a gem of entertainment nestled in the Smokies. It was built by the beloved Dolly Parton, who envisioned it as a park that could be enjoyed by impoverished children in the region, whose need for entertainment often falls under the radar. Parton herself grew up in rural Tennessee, gaining first-hand knowledge of how poverty and deprivation can squeeze the joy out of a child's life. Her literacy program for children in Appalachia is another example of her largesse. That said, Dollywood has been a site of trepidation for me since the first time I entered the gates.

Areas of the park are dressed in the style of 1950s-era America, with vintage diners and police cars that recall sock hops, soda jerks, and bobby socks. In other areas, customers will find old-time blacksmith and cooking stations selling vintage signs and freshly-cured pork rinds. Though I have seen other African Americans at the park on the several occasions I have been, they are few and far between.

Nostalgia for black people comes with the baggage of race history. The South in the '50s for African Americans meant segregation. Many of the diners that looked like the very ones standing in Dollywood would not have catered to blacks as customers. It is difficult to casually saunter through this terrain and feel comfortable munching a candy apple.

As I walked along the path with my stepchildren bouncing on their toes while considering which rollercoaster to ride next, I cheered myself by thinking this might be a good moment for a photo. Looking around, I noticed one of those large wooden stands with cut-out faces people can poke their heads through to suddenly look like they are dressed in '50s garb. I noticed that, in this one, the figures were of a white man and a white woman with a wide skirt and blonde ringlets. I immediately looked around for one that might better reflect my daughter's brown skin and hair, but there wasn't one. I let the photo idea drop and watched my little one trail her hand along the painted surface of the stand before finding something else to occupy her attention. I sighed with relief as we exited the gates two hours later, thinking that there are many ways people can let you know that a place is not for you.

Later, we stopped at one of our favorite barbeque eateries and, as chance would have it, our waiter ended up being a "good ol' boy" who introduced himself as Wrangler. I gave him a double-take when he announced his name, and he affirmed that, indeed, it was his actual name. When he brought over our waters, my husband told our youngest to sit up so she wouldn't spill. The waiter casually stated, "Yeah, you better listen. What are you going to do when your teachers start carrying guns? You'll really have to listen then." Both of our kids looked up in horror as he cackled and walked away, pleased with his post-Parkland joke.

I titled this essay "Kissing Dixie Goodbye." It seems like a difficult endeavor when we are living during a time period when American populism appears to want to embrace the Dixie ethos, expand its borders, and never let it go again.

4

A Lynching in North Carolina

*I have my high school locker neighbor to thank
for indirectly educating me about the basics of
historical lynchings. One Halloween, he decided
to dress as a KKK Klansman and wore a white
hood and robe with a knotted rope slung over his
shoulder to our small Massachusetts high school.*

On the day that I find out that an African American
Hairston was lynched by 150 white men, one thought
is uppermost in my mind: to the man who took the time
to count the perpetrators, I would first like to say thank
you for being so thorough, and I hope that at some point
in the years after the lynching you thought about other
things you might have done in those long moments
before two black men were hanged from a tree before
your eyes and those of the other masked members of
the Ku Klux Klan.It was while reading *The Hairstons:*

An American Family in Black and White that I found out about the author's belief that one of my ancestors was lynched in 1881. The book traces the slave-owning history of the white Hairstons and the African Americans that they enslaved over the course of their participation in the United States slave trade. While both white and black individuals carry the name Hairston, based on their transgenerational relationships during slavery, black Hairstons—like a large number of ex-slaves—took on the name of their one-time enslavers after emancipation. Many of these previously enslaved persons were related based on familial plantation relationships, but many were not. My known relationship with lynching victim Estes Hairston is based on sharing a history of common ancestors once enslaved by the same European family.

I know the history of racial violence in America, and lynch law is an important part of that history, so why was I so galvanized by news of a once-enslaved ancestor being touched intimately by this very same history? Perhaps it was because of my own recent, twenty-first century involvement with Klan semiotics. There was the incident the previous spring semester when, while teaching in a college classroom in the South, I'd been forced to request that security excuse a student from the room for exhibiting the Confederate flag during class after I'd asked him to put it away, and he'd refused.

As he was walked out of the classroom and down the hall, he continued to explain that he was not a racist. I tried not to hear security responding "We know, we know," convincing myself that they were just trying to talk him down and that I should not read it as their weighing in with an opinion on the issue.

There was also the incident that had taken place the previous summer: I'd been invited to attend a tour of a Confederate cemetery on another college campus. I politely declined, and was left wondering why anyone might imagine that a black woman would want to walk among the tombstones of people who fought a war to keep her ancestors enslaved.

The Ku Klux Klan was established by ex-Confederate soldiers who needed to change their tactics for subjugating blacks after the Civil War did not result in secession from the Union. These disgruntled rebel soldiers continued to wage their own war beneath a hood and under the banner of the Confederate flag. When I see a Confederate flag today, that's the heritage I see being claimed and celebrated. So, after learning about the Estes Hairston lynching, it was not like looking back through history—it was more like looking across at a parallel history that continues to unfold upon the foundation of those Confederate stars and bars.

~

I have my high school locker neighbor to thank for indirectly educating me about the basics of historical lynchings. One Halloween, he decided to dress as a KKK Klansman and wore a white hood and robe with a knotted lynch rope slung over his shoulder to our small Massachusetts high school. If not for seeing him that day, a walking synecdoche for black death, I might have believed lynching was a historical anomaly.

At home I was taught not all white people will want to be friends with you. This was my parents' way of teaching black self-preservation in the racially hostile environment of our small New England town in the 80s. They knew we would face racism, but they did not want to call it out by name unless we had experienced it already. Instead, they hid their message in a coded phrase about friendship. Even though I knew my lockermate might not be my friend, he smiled at me every day and said hello. Then, one day, he came to school dressed as a Klansman while smiling and saying hello. Still, it was years before I was able to translate the phrase *not all white people will want to be friends with you* into *you must be careful because a smile can be a prelude to death as easily as an expression of joy*. Yes, as a young black girl living in America, I was taught to look for oppression or suppressed violence behind a smile. Sometimes I would look so hard my fellow classmates would accuse me of staring.

~

What I noticed initially as I read the first article detailing the North Carolina lynching deaths of Estes Hairston and his companion Ed Lindsey (also Lindsay) by the Ku Klux Klan, was how the typeset words were a model of Jim Crow-era rhetoric. The stock phrase "both [men] charged with rape" is a well-worn refrain. This was the accusation frequently employed to justify the taking of a black life because of the explosive image it raised in the white male imagination: a cringing and weeping white woman beneath the hands and body of a depraved black man. Too often, during my scouring of historical records, I encountered this charge leveled against black men, because it was a convenient narrative that justified any level of violence perpetrated on the black body. So much so that, based on the degree of violence against black people in post-Reconstruction America, a black man was more likely to soil his pants at the sight of a white woman than be aroused by her. Which was, of course, the whole point of lynching; it was meant to terrorize and intimidate black men who sought to establish themselves economically and exert their newly-minted Constitutional civil rights as freedmen after the Civil War.

The article also pointed out the act of unlawful abduction: "[They] were taken from the jail and hanged about four miles from that place." In small rural towns, everything is close by—the jailhouse and the nearest lynch tree. Black bodies were stolen and brought to

America for servitude, and centuries later emancipation still did not keep them from being stolen from the jail-house and killed by an angry mob. Finally, the witnesses described, so large in number, were not present to quietly denounce the crime: "About one hundred and fifty men were engaged in the transaction." The jeering crowd was another hallmark of lynch law. There was safety in numbers. When men, women, and children gathered for a lynching, they could feel comforted by the fact that their neighbors believed as they did that the violence they would all soon witness was justified. As an aside, the reporter absolves the criminal mob of their crime: "We regret that this mode has to be resorted to in order to avenge wrong." This final newspaper statement, the feigned regret, serves to humanize the killers, but certainly not their victims.

The lynching of Estes and Lindsey was syndicated nationally. According to *The Western Sentinel* on June 23, 1881, under the header "Two Negro Rapists Lynched" "Estes Hairston, was charged with committing a rape upon a white girl twelve years of age . . . The other man, Lindsay, was charged with having committed the same crime upon a white woman." The two were then "taken from the jail by a party of one hundred and fifty men, and hanged." The reported facts of the charge often changed based on the publication printing them. *The Savannah Morning News* on June 24, 1881, referred to Estes as a man but Lindsay as a "colored boy" in prison for assault of not a woman but "two white girls," one of them "eight years [old]," who died from her injuries.

The inconsistent "facts" around Estes, Lindsey, and their reported victims was not unusual in such cases. The accusation alone by white males of an assault on a white woman was considered an admission of black guilt—details were secondary. Additionally, in the face of white male rage, the accusation was enough impetus for the murder of the accused. While token coverage of lynchings was common, and usually only took up a few lines of newspaper copy, larger discussions of lynching also took place in the press. These larger discussions were centered on why mobs of white men felt justified in breaking black men accused of crimes out of prison and hanging them.

A significant fact of the story that remains consistent in all media coverage is that Estes and Lindsey were held for seven months before being abducted from prison by a mob intent on their murder. The timeframe of imprisonment alone was meant to protect and preserve their lives for a fair trial that never took place; this was a trial promised to them as a post-Emancipation right guaranteed by the Fourteenth Amendment. The perspective of the lynchers, however, was that blacks were not entitled to a trial because the legal system failed to execute enough of them when they were charged with any type of crime. Lynchers could not accept that this absolute form of capital punishment without a formal hearing was an antebellum anachronism. The perspective of the lynchers was closely tied to slave-era law regarding African Americans. During slavery, an enslaved person could neither question nor look a white person in the eye upon penalty of death. This was the level of control white males were used to, and this is what they still expected in post-Emancipation America. The threat of constitutionally guaranteed civil rights with a fair trial for black men was seen by would-be lynchers as much too generous. As a consequence, mob lynchings provided a more agreeable outcome.

This news event, and the catalyst for it, could easily have sprung from African American journalist Ida B. Wells-Barnett's *The Red Record,* her important treatise on lynch history published in 1895. In her short but impactful study, Wells-Barnett uses her journalistic skills to outline the crisis of African American lynchings in America as presented in national newspapers and her own research from 1892–94. The results corroborate the ritualistic killing of black men, women, and children by white mobs often comprised of men, women, and children. I quote excerpts from Wells-Barnett on the killing of Lee Walker, who was hanged and then burned by such a mob, as evidence of lynch behaviors: "One man and woman brought a little girl, not over twelve years old, apparently their daughter, to view a scene which was calculated to drive sleep from the child's

eyes for many nights." In regard to the practice of col-
lecting souvenirs in the same case, Wells-Barnett states:
"The rope that was used to hang the Negro, and also that
which was used to lead him from jail, were eagerly sought by
relic hunters . . . Others of the relic hunters remained
until the ashes cooled to obtain such ghastly relics as the
teeth, nails, and bits of charred skin of the immolated
victim" (59). Wells-Barnett makes the point that the data
she uses was largely compiled by the white press, the
stories already in national distribution before she wrote
about them in *The Red Record*. She emphasizes that
these were crimes committed against the African American community in plain sight, because the perpetrators
had no fear of ever being charged. The murders of Estes
and Lindsey took place in 1881, a time period prior to
the turn of the century, which was considered the nadir
of African American postbellum race struggle. This was
during the same timeframe that Wells-Barnett chronicles.
According to one Hairston family plantation record, it
appears that Estes was born a slave in 1858. After emancipation, according to census record, he moved into a
household with his brother in Stokes County, North
Carolina, and worked as a farm laborer. The Southern
violence of these years against newly freed slaves, still
living under lowly social conditions, led to the Great
Migration of blacks fleeing the racial violence of the
South for the relative safety of the North.

~

It was during the "Without Sanctuary" exhibit in New York City in the 1990s that I first learned about the post-cards that were generated to commemorate the practice of lynching. I remember waiting in line at the New York Historical Society, along with a crush of people of all races, to view the historical memorabilia. The space was small, so those in attendance shuffled along as politely as they could in order to have a few minutes to glimpse the horrific images of dead and distorted black bodies displayed before jeering mobs. A keyword search of the exhibit title will still bring up an online version of these images. The muted, sepia tones of early photography remain powerful. The states the cards hail from are numerous and include California, Texas, Georgia, Oklahoma, Kansas, Alabama, Minnesota, Indiana, Montana, Kentucky, Nebraska, Illinois, Tennessee, Florida, West Virginia, Ohio, Missouri, and Louisiana. The years covered are lengthy, ranging from 1878–1960.

For me, these photographs represented a different kind of souvenir. Previously, I had only read of the hair, fingers, toes, ears, and genitalia of hanged black men being squirreled away as keepsakes after lynchings. These postcards were something new. As I moved through the exhibit, I thought about the many cities I had traveled to on holidays, purchasing postcards of local sites to send to friends and family to share my joyful experiences and give them insight into my embrace of a world larger than myself. Now, standing before yellowed postcards of tortured black men, I could not wrap my mind around the level of depravity necessary for someone to gloat over a disfigured body and share that as an endearing moment in their life. Simultaneously, the thought struck me that a person could only do this if they thought of blacks as inhuman, and something only to be prized in death. In these photographs, the black body became a staged hunting trophy with the great white hunters after the kill.

It is one of the many ironies of history that the perpetrators of violence are never able to avoid gloating over what they consider their would-be victories. For example, often after watching French filmmaker Alain Resnais's Holocaust documentary *Night and Fog* (1956) in class, my students will ask where all of this archival film footage of the Holocaust came from. I will then explain that, along with the newsreels taken by Allied forces during the liberation of the camps, the Nazis kept very careful records. They indicted themselves, and these indictments were, of course, corroborated by living witnesses. Similarly, the trophy photographs commemorating fetishistic lynch murders became another record of the diabolic public executions of black men and women.

Legislatively, the mailing of lynching postcards through the U.S. Postal Service was addressed by the federal government in the early twentieth century.

In 1908, an article under the headline "Bar Lynching Postcards: Texas Inspectors Close Mails to Represen- tations of White Domination" out of Austin, Texas, claimed: "The Post Office Department through local inspectors to-day barred from mails postcard pictures of negro lynchings. The particular card which brought about this ruling had on it the picture of the five negroes hanging on a tree lynched last July in Sabine county during the race disturbance there." It turns out that the problematic aspect of the card that led to the ban was the following tagline, which appeared under the photograph of the five lynch victims: "An emblem of white suprem- acy; A lesson taught in the white man's school; That this is the land of the white man's rule." To give some idea of the regional breadth of the practice, a similar announce- ment out of Hopkinsville, KY on August 19, 1908, under the headline "Can't Mail Lynch Views: Collectors Must Fill Post-Card Albums with Less Gruesome Pictures" reads: "Postmaster Breathitt was officially informed that postcards mailed out of Hopkinsville and other towns recently, showing the four bodies of negroes lynched at Russellville, August 1, should not have been allowed to pass thru (sic) Uncle Sam's hands."

The history of lynching in America is a thick and complex web of violence. The National Memorial for Peace and Justice in Montgomery, Alabama, was com- pleted in 2018 as a public recognition of the more than 4,400 victims of raced lynchings in the United States.

The memorial exhibit faithfully depicts the most common public and private reasons for lynchings, which included African Americans trying to register to vote; actually casting their votes; contradicting the word of a white person; talking to a white woman; being accused of the rape of a white woman; defending the assault of a black woman by a white man; threatening the body of a white person; or being accused of taking the life of a white person. The memorial also provides a sacred space for all Americans to better understand the violent nature of racially motivated mob violence against African Americans well into the twentieth century.

In the summer of 2018, I finally visited The National Memorial for Peace and Justice, waiting since the spring of that year when the memorial was first opened, to find out if a marker with the names of Estes and Lindsey had been erected there. When I first saw the marker with their names etched into steel, I felt a sense of relief that they had not been relegated to a forgotten moment in history. Their lynching story of being stolen from prison by a raging mob, however, was not unique. It was a regular practice for lynchers to break their intended victims out of prison under the very noses of prison guards. In frustration, one judge affirmed in 1887 after such a breakout that he would no longer waste the court's time trying to convict lynchers because the juries in such cases would rarely convict the guilty parties.

On a June night in 1881, Estes and Lindsey were

abducted from prison, where they had resided for seven months, by the KKK. Recently, news had been circulating that the young girl who had been assaulted seven months previous had died, and the woman who had been raped was missing. According to the assembled mob, this meant that a fair trial could not take place if there were no witnesses, so they took matters into their own hands.

~

How does the history of lynching affect black people? I cannot speak for all black people, but the effects are often unpredictable. James Byrd was lynched in Jasper, Texas, in 1998. He was offered a ride by three white men on that day and, instead of taking him to where he wanted to go, they chained him to the back of their pickup truck and dragged his body until he was decapitated. It is difficult to describe feral hate to people who have not experienced it. You see, James Byrd knew at least one of his killers. I was haunted by the smile that he was probably offered with that ride, the gleaming white teeth and parted lips a well-disguised rictus of venom. As I read about his death, I relived each moment in my imagination. The brutal beating that turned him into a compliant body. The heavy rattle of chains that brought him back to consciousness as he realized what was going to happen. The revving of the truck's engine followed by the whoop of rebel yells. The first jerk of pain when the chains tightened and his body scraped the road as the truck accelerated and spewed a blast of exhaust into his face. I relived each moment so that he did not have to die alone. Empathy made me a witness to the loss of a human being, not the monster his murderers had made him out to be in their own skewed imaginations.

When I first read Harlem Renaissance writer Countee Cullen's *The Black Christ* (1929), a book-length poem about lynching, I visccrally understood the powcr of serving as a witness for the dead, and the necessary commitment to social justice. Reflecting on the work of this kindred literary spirit governed my own decision to preface my first poem about lynching with an epigraph from *The Black Christ*:

> *I shoved him in a closet set*
> *Against the wall. This would but let*
> *Him breathe two minutes more, or three,*
> *Before they dragged him out to be*
> *Queer fruit upon some outraged tree.*

My poem on lynching was written years before I found out about Estes Harriston's lynching in 1881. I was just being a good student of history. It was a creative acknowledgement of those who had lived through the nascent, violent phases of black civil rights in America, and the witnesses who knew that the end of slavery in America was going to come with a price that would be exacted long after the last soldier was removed from the Civil War battlefield.

After re-reading my poem and one of the news articles on the lynching, I realized that I had possibly written an elegy for a tortured ancestor years before I even knew his name. In retrospect, the poem was an answer to his prayer to survive that went unanswered that night, when the only other black man in attendance was the one who was hanged alongside him.

Dying By the Rood

I can only wonder what it was like
a man, a tree, and history.
After fear comes a determined resignation.
Just ask anyone who has given birth,
said goodbye to a lover too soon,
finally accepted the creep of old age,
or seen life flash before them
in a heart-stopping moment.

I can only imagine that final stretch
pale palm raised to ask for help,
praying that God would call out one
among these white faces
to raise his voice and say
Naw boys, y'all go on home now,

we're not going to do this tonight.
And you would accept the apology,
allow the rope to slip over your head
and drop from your wrists,
head home for supper like nothing had
ever happened, wiping the blood from
your shattered face with a grateful sleeve.

Instead, the slow creep of grim acceptance
that your name was not Isaac
and there would be no ram
in the bush to make
this executioner's noose pass over you.

With no voice left, your mind alone screams
that you'd never even looked
at that white woman.
Would never
touch another woman period
if you could only walk away.

Still, something compels you to look up.
Maybe if your eyes could only reach heaven
that man after the order of Melchizedek
would hear your prayer
and release this last breath stuck
in your lungs, keep your bound knuckles
from scraping this tree.

5

PULL AND DRAG

I have to confess that my own aquatic skills came about through a mix of parental responsibility and federal desegregation.

I rarely see any people of color swimming in my gym pool in Knoxville, Tennessee. I always imagine that people are amazed to see me doing laps. Most of them probably believe that black people can't swim and I'm just a cultural anomaly. I say this because just recently I caught another article in the news about the high number of African Americans who acknowledge not being able to swim—a number much higher than other racial groups on national average. My gut twisted when I read it, in that way that most people experience when they realize they have risen above a statistic, but know that this does not make the statistic incorrect. I have to confess that my own aquatic skills came about through a mix of parental responsibility and federal desegregation.

I came to understand the importance of learning to swim when, as a youngster, I was thrown into the deep end of a community pool by an older cousin's boyfriend. The only reason I can figure he did this was because he had a sick sense of humor. After all, no one in our little group knew how to swim at the time. From the bottom of the pool, I looked up through rippling waters sharply illuminated by a summer sun and watched the horrified face of my cousin contort with fear as she screamed to anyone listening, "She can't swim!" When no one immediately came to my rescue, she bravely walked the two steps she could before sliding down into the deep end herself, grabbed my wrist, and tugged me back into shallow water.

I don't remember my cousin and this particular boyfriend dating much longer after that incident. I do remember in those few seconds on the bottom of the pool, during which I contemplated the death that would surely come as soon as I took a deep breath of freshly chlorinated water, I had an epiphany: I must learn to swim.

My journey toward swimming competency began when my family purchased a house with a pool in Coral Gables, Florida. Like most people with pools, my parents did not think it wise to have one with a houseful of kids who could not swim. My dad knew how to swim and he volunteered to teach us. At the time, I was the only one who trusted him enough to learn. After a brief demonstration of the dog paddle, he simply swam out to the center of the pool and told me to swim to him. He waited expectantly, water weighing down his large afro into bangs and waved *come on* with his arms in encouragement. I was young enough at the time to think it was a cute game and mimicked what he had done, and *voila*! From then on, I showed off my dog paddle to anyone who asked if I could swim.

My parents' migration from South Florida to a predominantly white New England suburb in western Massachusetts in the late 1970s was supposed to be a privilege. We kids were often told how lucky we were to be in such a good, Northern school system. My parents came of age during segregation and still held vivid memories of old, second-hand schoolbooks inherited from the nearby white schools in their respective rural Florida hometowns. In their minds, Brown v. Board of Education and the "Little Rock Nine" of high school integration fame had fought the battle of walking the gauntlet of jeering faces and racial epithets barked from angry mouths. This was proof that our rambling colonial home had been bought with a price, and that price had already been paid. Racism, however, can cross regional borders. I often wondered if they would have been shocked to know that, when I walked the streets of our quaint town to my ballet class or home from school, I could count on hearing a rebel yell and the n-word emanating from a car full of teenagers. While I faced rampant racism in my school and town, I was able to capitalize on at least one aspect of attending a school in a community with money: an indoor pool.

I give my New England high school the lion's share of credit for ensuring that I avoided aquatic profiling. Our school instituted a standard requirement that no student be allowed to graduate without first passing a swim and lifesaving water safety test. The only way to avoid this requirement was a dire medical excuse. In fact, the only time you would see students warming the bleachers during gym class at the pool was when girls were on their periods. They acted like they didn't feel the envious glances sliding their way as the rest of us plunged into frigid water while the snow fell outside during a typical northeastern winter. Of course, the rest of us ladies hated them, knowing that our hair would still be wet when we stepped gingerly across the icy pathways to the waiting buses after the dismissal bell, trying desperately to get on before our hair had time to harden against the cold.

The hair. In one way or another, swimming for those with genetically-challenging coifs always ends up being about the hair. Over the years I have learned how to work my black-girl hair to accommodate my love of the water. When long, I can handily manipulate it into a smoothly-gelled ponytail or bun. When short, I simply use the same gel after a swim and immediately wrap it in a scarf for 30 minutes to fix in nice water waves.

Think Duke Ellington.

Alas, black mothers often pass on their fear of the water to their daughters via the upkeep of their hair. In my youth, I remember my stepmother trying a multitude of swimming caps to keep our hair dry. She had three girls, and doing hair could end up consuming half a day. The caps, of course, never worked. No matter how snug, the pool water would always sneak beneath the taut rubber, converting our straight locks back to curly kink. The average chemical relaxer (aka hair straightener) at a hairdresser can cost anywhere from $65–$100 including tip. A flat-ironed hairstyle is not much cheaper and only lasts as long as water and humidity are kept at bay. Mothers are loath to pay those prices and then let their kids go swimming on Saturday and have nothing to work with on Sunday morning before church. It may sound superficial and unbelievable, but this is the reason many black women shun both the pool and gym workouts that make one sweat profusely. I can honestly say I never questioned nor regretted my desire for health over hair.

The goal of the swim program was not only to ensure every graduating senior knew how to swim but that they were also proficient enough to save the life of someone who didn't. With only a dog paddle under my belt, I was immediately thrown into the novice group, where I spent my time going across the width of the pool and mastering the required strokes: freestyle, backstroke, breaststroke, and sidestroke. I did this until I was able to complete a lap of each stroke, in proper form, along the length of the pool. This, however, was not the end of the proficiency training.

A "pass" for the high school graduation requirement included swimming twenty laps while alternating strokes. Not only was the pool of high school competitive length, it was also competitive diving depth. In order not to flounder, I had to seriously pace myself to meet the challenge. I did it, but had no time for a pat on the back before putting on clothes for the final requirement.

The life-saving component of the test required students jump into the deep end of the pool fully clothed and turn the clothing we had on into flotation devices. Who could have known how tight jeans get when they are wet, or how difficult they were to peel off and then fling overhead until they filled with air to prove that you were able to stay afloat atop the now bloated legs? Ditto for a long-sleeved button-down shirt. After this herculean feat, I treaded water for five minutes to finish out the requirement; in fact, it was a relief.

Now I understood what it meant to know how to swim. I was proud of my achievement, but didn't think much of it beyond the fact that I could now graduate.

In my post-high school life, I was amazed by the number of contexts in which knowing how to swim gave me access to all kinds of possibilities just because I was no longer seen as a liability. I could readily accept invitations to go swimming in lakes without having to touch the murky bottoms. When I was invited to pool parties, I could actually swim instead of merely sitting on the side of the pool and dangling my legs in the water. Thankfully, I was not one of those girls trapped into trying to look nonchalant after a visit to the hairdresser and praying that no one would splash a new hairdo into an unstyled afro.

Knowing how to swim even helped my dating life once I reached adulthood. On a weekend Caribbean getaway to the Bahamas with family, I met a local guy at a bar. I wasn't much into hitting the casino, so he promised to take me boating and snorkeling around the island. My new tour guide said he would pick me up in his boat after he got off work.

Waiting on the beach later, I wondered how close he would come to shore to pick me up. I imagined myself running along the sand in my chic string bikini until I completed a shallow dive into the waves, emerged like a sea nymph from below, and lightly treaded water to get my bearings before I glided into a competent crawl toward the boat. When my date pulled up quite a few yards from shore, I was easily able to make the swim out to the boat. Later he took me deep-water shelling for conch, and I didn't have a care beyond running into a shark in the crystal-clear waters. None of this would have been possible without learning to swim.

After I gave birth to my oldest daughter, within a few

months I made sure she had her first ocean experience. At the time, I was advised that the salt water at the beach would make her newborn skin peel. One look at that gummy smile when my child saw her first waves break onto shore made me ignore that warning. Feet tapping wavelets as I held her hands, I saw her laugh with delight for the first time.

At the age of three, this same daughter requested I teach her to swim. Feeling completely empowered, I worked with her until she mastered the trick of simultaneously holding her breath and floating motionless atop the water, her dreadlocks spreading out like a fan around her small head. I then demonstrated the powerful cupped palm that was the secret to the water-liberating dog paddle. From there, I watched her refine her technique until she mastered the underwater breaststroke that became her credential to attend pool parties and enjoy luxurious swims in water over her head. I felt an amazing sense of achievement in teaching my daughter how to swim. In truth, I had given her a second gift of life; like learning to ride a bicycle, she would never unlearn her ability to navigate through water.

A couple of years ago I went to the community pool in our Knoxville suburb with my five-year-old stepdaughter. She was excited that there was another child in the pool and smiled at him to encourage a greeting; however, we were both stunned when he turned to his grandmother and said, "She's brown. Why is she here?" Most millennials may not know that public swimming pools were once segregated. There is a scene in the biopic *Introducing Dorothy Dandridge* (1999), based on the life of the African American actress, that shows Halle Berry as Dorothy Dandridge dipping a toe into the segregated pool of the Las Vegas Frontier Hotel. Apparently, Dandridge did this as an act of resistance after being told that management would have to drain and clean the pool if she, being a black woman, got into it. This took place in the 1950s, yet here was a child in 2014, who was only four years old, asking why a brown girl was in his community swimming pool. While the desegregation of public pools might not be widely taught as a part of race history, certainly discrimination had been introduced to this young man's consciousness from somewhere.

Standing beside the floatie-encased arms of her grandson, the boy's grandmother had the decency to blush at her grandson's indiscretion. If I were quick enough, I might have responded in that sickly-sweet voice people adopt when really pushed to the edge that "We are here because our housing association dues afford this black family the right to be here." Instead, I did the diplomatic thing and proceeded to talk to the grandmother about the importance of young people learning how to swim. I then turned away and proceeded to teach my step-daughter how to cup her palms and pull them through the water as she stood on the second stair of the pool, her neatly braided wet hair glistening under the penetrating sunlight. Her movement was a proclamation: I belong here.

6

CHILDHOOD KEEPSAKES

The dried sage had been carefully bound with red silk ribbon. The gift was reasuring and made everyone feel confident they had facilitated a small, but very real, historical corrective.

On a beautiful late summer day in a small, northeastern Pennsylvania town, members of my husband's family have gathered to deliver Native American artifacts that have been in his family for approximately seventy years into the hands of curators at a local Native American museum. The artifacts belonged to his grandfather who once, according to family lore, enjoyed a relationship with local Native American tribal leaders. The story goes that some of these artifacts were gifted in recognition of his work as a Boy Scout leader. In his role as troop founder, he devoted some time to educating young men about nineteenth-century American history and culture in the Pennsylvania region in the 1920s and '30s. I, however, learned about the beaded moccasins, feathered headdresses, tobacco pouch, pink-beaded headband, and other articles in casual conversation with my husband. Without thinking about it I commented, "You know, you should give them back." My suggestion was a default reaction to all I knew of colonial settler exploitation of Native Americans. The words positing a return of traditional objects, however, flew out of my mouth before I even considered the specifics of back to whom. Now, two years after my casual comment, we were preparing to do just that.

The family knew nothing of these artifacts other than the stories the pieces themselves told through their physical bearing. We would never know if the beaded strip of light pink satin had been worn as a headband by any child other than my husband's sandy-haired sister, or if the feathered headdresses had adorned crowns other than his own family's during childhood nights trick-or-treating at Halloween, when neighbors marveled at their authenticity. The provenance of each piece, from drum to pipe bag, had died with my husband's grandfather, a one-time collector hobbyist. Still, with more confidence than the situation probably warranted, we bundled everything up into four plastic storage tubs, only to reopen them in a museum an hour and a half later like an off-season Christmas gift exchange.

As we stood awkwardly in front of the Lenape elder

who opened the tubs, we actually found out more about the pedigree of the articles than we could have surmised on our own. Perhaps the biggest surprise of all was that the items were of western Plains tribal origin, and not native to Pennsylvania at all. As the elder took out one of the headdresses, he opened it in the way it would appear if worn, and my breath caught at how majestic it suddenly appeared. Now I understood why it had garnered so much attention during my husband's youth when he sported it around his suburban neighborhood. No longer lying on its side and shuttered in a box, it looked like its only appropriate setting was at a powwow.

Even though the family lore of provenance was proven wrong, what we did get right was that the pieces were appreciated, because we were told as much. In return, the family was given a traditional sage smudge bundle. It was the type of bundle used to ceremonially dispel bad spirits. The dried sage had been carefully bound with red silk ribbon. The gift was reassuring and made everyone feel confident they had facilitated a small, but very real, historical corrective.

I have often facilitated moments of cultural reconciliation in the classroom through lecture and discussion, but this rekoning with family keepsakes was new territory for me. The exchange moved pedagogy from theory within the four walls of the classroom into real-world practice.

~

It is the start of a new semester after our summer gift exchange. On the first day of one of my contemporary multiracial literature courses, I pause to ask students, "How many of you have read a book by a Native American author?" This is not the first time I have asked this question and, as usual, the answer is zero. With a little prodding, some students admit to rumored romantic threads of Native American blood flowing through their familial gene pool: the tale of a great-great-grandmother believed to be Cherokee passed down as the oral remains of blood ties lost through subsequent monoracial couplings.

Admittedly, their stories are not new to me, because they resemble my own. I also hold onto the memory of the creased photograph my own mother once showed me as a child of her Aunt Sallie: a Cherokee woman whose hair was long enough to sit on. The grainy black and white photo revealed a tanned woman looking stoically into the camera's eye, dressed in black. Still, all things being unequal, the construct of racial reality revealed my family, among them some of her descendants, were African American to the naked eye, and so we married from generation to generation maintaining that genealogical line.

In the United States, race is the way you look, live, and walk in your life. This is the ground zero where

I start to deconstruct romanticized histories with my students. I am quick to point out to a student admitting to a fractional amount of Native blood buried in their family tree that, despite this reality, they are not walking a Native American walk in their public life. I also note that this, however, does not invalidate their value as a cultural ally; allyship is not built on the vestiges of romance—it is concrete. It begins, instead, with pages glued into a spine and graced with a cover that elaborate on the American historical record.

It is November 8, 2018, and I am preparing another American literature lecture for my English majors. We have been reading Layli Long Soldier's poetry collection *Whereas* (2017), and this morning I have decided to start the class by listening to podcasts featuring the first two Indigenous women ever elected to Congress on November 6, 2018: Sharice Davids and Debra Haaland.

I cue up a TED Talk with Haaland titled "Who Speaks for You" and watch my students absorb the facts of the congresswoman's family history, which includes her father and mother serving in the United States Marines and Navy. This is a jarring transhistorical switch from the historical record of United States armed forces corralling Native Americans and marching them across the country in 1831 that we read about as part of the Indian Removal Act. Haaland's twenty-first century narrative highlights a familial, military veteran status. For Americans, this is an irrefutable stamp of national identity, because it involves laying down one's life as a patriot for one's countrymen. There is no denying that two events—the Indian Removal Act and Haaland's congressional election—were predated by first-contact skirmishes between English settlers and Indigenous Americans along the Massachusetts shoreline. One version of this history was documented by William Bradford in his travelogue *Of Plymouth Plantation* (1651) in the seventeenth century. I had taken my students through Bradford's penned lines excusing the violence of colonization as a divine call to settle America by any means necessary. The story, however, did not stop there.

Next, we followed the forced migration of Eastern band tribes westward under President Andrew Jackson's administration. Jackson's policy of removal was a deliberate acquiescence to settler concerns over their safe westward expansion across historic Native lands. This agrarian idealism, so admired by President Thomas Jefferson, dictated that the best people were those who worked the land to provide for their families. According to Jefferson, this landedness would prevent settlers from concerning themselves with the affairs of their neighbors and cultivate a climate of peace among men. With Native Americans removed from the land by the United States government, these romanticized European pioneers could settle new towns and homestead at will, realizing their agrarian, American dream at the cost of Indigenous displacement.

Our discussion concluded with the details of Native American boarding schools created to finally erase the cultural legacy of Indigenous people on the American landscape. Devoid of land and culture, it would be just a matter of time before Native Americans were completely assimilated into European cultural norms. The tools of this final level of assimilation included: preventing boarding school students from speaking their native languages, wearing their traditional clothes, and even their traditional hairstyles by cutting off their hair. This controlled genocide, termed colonialism, was the price paid by Native Americans to finally be allowed entry into the American body politic.

On this post-election Thursday in November 2018, my students also contemplate Davids's political platform in a local television interview, where she espouses new gun laws and comprehensive healthcare. It does not escape their notice that both Davids and Haaland speak with confidence in their new role at the vanguard of twenty-first century American politics. In particular, I call attention to Davids's use of the pronoun "our" in reference to the United States and fellow Americans who share her values for the nation, because I know how hard colonialism worked to ensure that "our" would never be used to indicate unity across American race lines. Yet, against all odds, these two Native American women outlived the ill-intended plot of history.

Returning to Long Soldier's collection *Whereas*, I

describe the etymology of the whereas statement as a term used to establish a legal precedent. While doing research on my own family genealogy in America, I encountered a legal statute handed down by King George of England in 1680:

> *WHEREAS the frequent meeting of considerable numbers of negroe slaves under pretence of feasts and burialls is judged of dangerous consequence; for prevention whereof for the future, Bee it enacted by the kings most excellent majestie by and with the consent of the generall assembly, and it is hereby enacted by the authority aforesaid, that from and after the publication of this law, it shall not be lawfull for any negroe or other slave to carry or arme himselfe with any club, staffe, gunn, sword or any other weapon of defence or offence . . .*

This historical pronouncement is a reminder that American slavery only worked by design, and designedly unarmed slaves were less of a threat than armed slaves. The poetry collection *Whereas*, however, conceptualizes disarmament from another perspective. In this case, it takes the form of an open apology engineered to disarm the expectations of the recipient. The genesis of the work was the 2010 Congressional Apology to Native Americans for generations of mistreatment under the guise of European colonialism. The opening lines read as follows:

*To acknowledge a long history of official depredations
and ill-conceived policies by the Federal Government
regarding Indian tribes and offer an apology to all Native
Peoples on behalf of the United States.*

*Whereas the ancestors of today's Native Peoples inhab-
ited the land of the present-day United States since time
immemorial and for thousands of years before the arrival
of people of European descent;*

*Whereas for millennia, Native Peoples have honored, pro-
tected, and stewarded this land we cherish;*

*Whereas Native Peoples are spiritual people with a deep
and abiding belief in the Creator, and for millennia Native
Peoples have maintained a powerful spiritual connection
to this land, as evidenced by their customs and legends;*

*Whereas the arrival of Europeans in North Amer-
ica opened a new chapter in the history of Native
Peoples . . . (S.J. Res. 14)*

A member of the Oglala Lakota Nation, Long Soldier
acknowledges in deft verse that an apology is merely
a reminder of what an underserved population recog-
nized as injustice all along. Indeed, apologies can be a
murky business. After all, it was an African American
man, President Barack Obama, who processed the

congressional apology on behalf of a nation that once enslaved both Indigenous Americans and Africans. This complex brush stroke reminds us all that the racial ironies of history often speak volumes.

I read my first Native-authored novel in the '90s. It was Leslie Marmon Silko's *Ceremony* (1977). The fragmented yet simple language of the diction resonated deeply with me. *Here was a writer*, I thought to myself, *I could identify with*. I lived for hyper-imagistic, simple lines of spare prose—the kind of writing that gave a reader time to think about the big picture between lines— and that is what she offered. This was also around the time that I was introduced to Chickasaw/Choctaw actor and activist Cochise Anderson. I believe he had only recently completed Julie Dash's film *Daughters of the Dust* (1991). Dash's *Daughters* reads as a series of intimate turn-of-the-century vignettes of an African American family residing on St. Helena Island off the coast of Georgia and South Carolina and contemplating immigration to the mainland. The story is rendered into breathtaking art by cinematographer Arthur Jafa. Anderson's role in the film is representative of the Native American presence in the South Sea Isles. In a highly stylized romantic scene he whisks away one of the African-descended Sea Island daughters to live among his people. The role was importantly representative and documented the historical connection between blacks and Native Americans in the region, but the screentime was deceptively brief.

I remember engaging in conversation with Anderson about the role and his joy over the cultural representation at the time. As a follow up, however, he also talked about the lack of more evolved roles for Native people in Hollywood—a problem that has not changed much in the decades since that conversation. In fact, I still screen the film *Smoke Signals*, written by Sherman Alexie, as a filmic accompaniment to contemporary Indigenous American fiction and poetry. More than twenty years out, it resonates with millennials who have grown up on Hollywood fodder that does not feature Native Americans in leading roles, and who often have Disney's *Pocahontas* as a racial reference point for Native Americans, past and present, on the big screen.

The importance of my husband's story of returned artifacts, for him, was that some particulars of his family history were incorrect, and an unexpected source had moved him closer to the truth. Taking a broader perspective, embedded in this story is a reminder that looking deeper can always bear greater fruit and add to the details of our collective American legacy.

7

WHEN I SAY AFRICA, YOU SAY . . .

American perceptions of Africa have not changed much in the past century based on a lack of new knowledge.

I was recently surprised in an undergraduate literature class when students accused the children in Zimbabwean novelist NoViolet Bulawayo's *We Need New Names* (2014) of being morally corrupt. This was their assessment after reading about the kids stealing guavas from trees in a wealthy white suburb in order to stave off hunger. The children were members of families relocated under President Mugabe's regime during the 1980s. Along with their parents, they were ousted from their middle-class homes only to struggle for survival in barely livable camp housing—effectively made refugees in their own nation. No, the trees they pilfered from were not their own, but, while reading, I had marveled at the survival skills of these children. Truthfully, I would have done the same, because there is nothing cute about hunger or being dispossessed. Yet, as I listened to my students debate the point, I was really struck in the moment by what appeared to be a lack of empathy for this set of starving kids. I could not help wondering if the judgmental attitude sprung from the fact that these were down-and-out African kids living in impoverished conditions instead of two middle-class white American children living in the bucolic countryside and sneaking over a fence to pick some of Farmer Brown's apples. In this version of the scene, the middle-class white youth might not have been starving, maybe just hungry with a one-or-two-hours-before-dinner hunger; not hungry in that I-have-not-eaten-in-twelve-or-more-hours-and-I-cannot-take-it-anymore way that triggers the body to move into survival mode. This latter hunger, in its most extreme manifestation, is the type viewers are treated to during late-night infomercials of the swollen bellies of African children with sunken eyes surrounded by buzzing flies. I have recently heard this late-night video footage crudely referred to as "poverty porn." This is a view of Africa that reduces it to a troubled country in the American imagination instead of a vast continent full of people from various class backgrounds.

American perceptions of Africa have not changed much in the past century based on a lack of new knowledge being circulated in traditional public school curriculums. When I ask students whether they have ever read an African novel, most claim they have not, or that they have read Joseph Conrad's *Heart of Darkness* (1902), if they were in an honors or AP English course in high school. The primary issue with stating that they have read *Heart of Darkness* is that it was written by a Polish-British author, not an African. Additionally, the fact that the novel was written about turn-of-the-century colonialism in the Congo points out that even contemporary readers are comfortable with the Western colonial point of view of the uncivilized African. This is an image that parallels the equally damaging image of the modern African pictured in late-night infomercials. Beyond these limited depictions of Africans, news coverage of the continent often depicts it as a series of nations in poverty-based struggle as a result of religious divisions, corrupt politicians, drought, and food shortages. While these situations certainly are the very real experiences of many Africans, they do not represent the sum total of a continent. Inarguably, examining the artistic and literary production of a people provides a much clearer vision of their humanity than a limiting news cycle.

Novelist Chimamanda Ngozi Adichie regularly speaks frankly about people who have not been ready to receive stories of Africans that complicate their own limited point of view. In her popular TED talk "The Danger of a Single Story," she relates an anecdote of her conversation with one of her professors, a man who said her novel *Americanah* (2013) was not "authentically African" because her "characters were too much like him: an educated and middle-class man." In his mind, there were no such people as upwardly-mobile Africans who attended prestigious colleges abroad and actually exercised agency over their lives versus being global victims. Writers write the stories they want to tell, but readers have to read broadly in order to not fall prey to the exploitation narrative as an everyman's story.

At some point, I imagine that all African Americans consider their relationship to the continent of Africa. For many it might begin and end with images of chained Africans departing from Gorée Island. Or, to be fair, maybe this view has been given a facelift by the arrival of newcomers like America's latest Kenyan-Mexican media darling, actress Lupita Nyong'o. Her acting talents are considerable and have earned her a recent starring roles in the film *Black Panther* (2018), Jordan Peele's *US* (2019), and a 2014 Academy Award for Best Supporting Actress in the film *12 Years a Slave*. Yet, in one of the ironies of Hollywood, the award came for her riveting performance as a Southern plantation slave.

After viewing *12 Years A Slave*, I had one of those awkward exchanges with a white woman in the movie theater restroom. She looked at me with an emotionally drained face and said, "Amazingly powerful film, wasn't it?" There was nothing to do but mumble "Yes."

These exchanges after films about slavery, or similarly oppressive histories of black American life, are always trying. My frustration is that, like this woman, many people feel a cathartic emotionalism that reminds them that they care enough to know that slavery was wrong. I, however, feel fairly confident that after leaving the theater behind, it will not change their views about black people in real time. For example, would this woman go on to question her children about their knowledge of slave history and how they feel about African Americans today over dinner that night? If she holds an executive position at a company that has limited diversity, would this film make her think about what she could do to make those numbers more equitable across race lines? Or, would seeing the film remain just a powerful but fleeting cathartic memory? Everything about my experiences in the United States indicated it would.

My own psychological connection between Africa and slavery was made for me in a seventh-grade social studies classroom in western Massachusetts. This was the only day during the year when blacks were discussed as subjects in the classroom, and it was to detail the history of American slavery. I was the only black person in the class, and the total contributions of my people, serving as plantation slaves, became an opportunity for the whole class to stare at me with ridicule. To compound the frustration of the day, before class a classmate wandered over to the globe and planted his finger on the upper third of the continent of Africa pronouncing "Niger" like the racial slur, not the country, and followed his pronouncement by looking over at me and stating, "It's named after you. You should go back and live there." Two thoughts came into my head simultaneously; the first was that no one would name a country after an insult, and the other was that nowhere in my brain lodged the accurate pronunciation of this country because we'd never studied Africa in this history class. Damage done.

Africa did not cease to be a scar of shame in my psyche until graduate school. It was not until this point in my intellectual maturation that I had the opportunity to discover the literary wealth of a continent that would help me to link the plight of African Americans with Africans and the greater African diaspora. My pan-Africanist consciousness raising began under the tutelage of African film and culture scholar Manthia Diawara during my tenure at New York University. In my mind, Dr. Diawara was the urbane, suave, handsome Malian scholar come to the United States to correct the minds of intellectual Americans about Africa. From the first day to the last of that semester, I supped on every morsel of information that spilled from his mouth. In his classroom, I finally read at length Frantz Fanon, Wole Soyinka, Camara Laye, and Aimé Césaire, among others. These works, influenced by the literary movement *Negritude*, helped me make the vital connections between African and Caribbean colonization, and

African American slavery. One of the high points of my academic experience at NYU was having Dr. Diawara hood me during my Master's degree ceremony.

I found a practical use for this new knowledge about Africa when I began spending time with recent African émigrés while living in New York. My roommate was Ghanaian and this new African community seemed to spring up around her, absorbing me as well. As a group we began to cook together, and I listened to raucous debates between Ghanaians and Senegalese about the merits of preparing *mafe* (peanut stew) from scratch and whether a mortar and pestle were necessary items in the modern American kitchen. The meals were often simple, but the preparation elaborate. There was the chopping of root vegetables, which were placed in a bowl of water so that they might soften while a fresh whole bluefish was prepared for broiling, and someone was sent to secure precious palm oil. Of course, this took me back to my own childhood, watching my Southern-born parents dice potatoes into perfectly-shaped cubes to be soaked in preparation for the boiling that would eventually make them a fit foundation for mustard potato salad. This memory was followed by those involving the more staged holiday meals my parents prepared at Thanksgiving, where the merits of homemade cornbread for turkey stuffing were touted over the quicker Jiffy cornbread mix version. In that Brooklyn kitchen, hidden away in Bedford-Stuyvesant, I was reminded that cooking is one of those universal cultural experiences with a single end goal: enough good food for everyone in attendance to enjoy.

The other aspect of these meals that harkened back to my own childhood was the ease these particular African men displayed in the kitchen, buzzing like a small hive as they attempted to recall every step that their mothers had taken to prepare a meal "back home." My own grandmother was guilty of raising sons and grandsons who were adept in the kitchen. In my family, most of the men could cook better than the women—who were no slackers themselves.

I didn't dare to ask how long until dinner during these cross-cultural culinary experiences, but instead accepted the endless supply of strong black tea served in tiny cups and sweetened with what should have been considered too much sugar. Finally, around the communal pot of rice, lamb or fish, and vegetables, we all reached in with our right hands and commenced to feast.

It was amazing to have such an intimate cultural immersion experience in the United States—the kind that only living in a major city can offer. It even got to the point where I would not think of using anything other than traditional Wolof greetings and farewells at our regular gatherings. That said, it was not long before I wanted to bring my academic and social worlds closer together.

By chance, at the time these new friendships were

being solidified, I was working on a seminar paper as part of my master's program and decided to share some of my primary sources with my new Senegalese friends. The source material happened to be Senegalese film-maker Ousmane Sembène's films *Black Girl* (1966) and *Borom Sarret* (1963). When I brought the films over for viewing, I assumed that everyone would have seen them already and would respond to them nostalgically, perhaps recounting when they had first viewed them in a school classroom as youth. Imagine my surprise when everyone was riveted to their seats in the living room and talking in low whispers about never having seen the films at all. This delayed knowledge of the accomplishments of one of their Senegalese countrymen was the result of cultural hegemony, a byproduct of both colonialism and slavery. How many generations of American blacks had been through the experience of never knowing that ex-slaves had written books? That many blacks lived as free people in the United States for generations before emancipation? That black people in the nineteenth century graduated from colleges, including Harvard? That many blacks authored novels, nonfiction, and poetry in America from the eighteenth century to the present? My whole academic journey was based on trying to correct these sorts of omissions in my own storehouse of knowledge, but, unlike my diasporic compatriots, my recuperation of lost history had taken place in my homeland, not my adoptive nation.

The second most profound revelation from this classroom experience during my graduate years was my exposure to African male feminism through Sembène's films. While a case can be made for the significance of the strong African female voice in many of Sembène's films, two films in particular impacted my thoughts on how men can involve themselves in feminist projects as allies through various artistic mediums: *Black Girl* and *Moolaad*é (2004). For anyone who has never seen it, *Black Girl* is perhaps the most artistic critique of French colonialism ever made. It is incredibly nuanced and heartfelt. It is the story of an African maid who is hired in Senegal and travels with her white French host family to the French Riviera, only to be exploited in one of the most luxurious enclaves in the world. Its black and white frames sing with the passion of a young *auteur* determined to make his mark in the world. In this film, Sembène set himself up to spend a lifetime trying to achieve anything half as good—and he continued to meet the challenge.

The second film, *Moolaad*é, deals with the global issue of female genital mutilation (FGM). In this film, Sembène speaks to the very communities who perpetuate the practice: village men and female elders. While the procedure is known to still be practiced globally in places where it is also illegal, even in Western cities in Europe, the political impact of Sembène's position against the practice is tremendous.

I recall on one occasion, before we dipped into one of our communal meals, it was gently suggested by one of the Senegalese men present that I not sit legs crisscross, but instead stretch my legs out before me so that only my ankles separated slightly at the ends. As I was wearing pants, a quick thought flashed through my mind. I wondered if this was because a woman who had experienced genital circumcision would never sit crisscross. Or was it just another way of obscuring female genitalia—perhaps akin to the way my own father had corrected my manspread while wearing a dress on Sunday mornings before church when I was kid?

The backstory of my exposure to a complex discourse on circumcision was initiated by my experience with traditional African dance. African dance became a major touchstone for me that paralleled my introduction to African writers. Most of the dance instructors I took classes with in New York for several years hailed from Senegal and Guinea-Bissau. I loved the rhythm of the drums, and the dance step combinations were somewhat accessible to me after my years of ballet and jazz. Most of the instructors were first-generation immigrants, so translation was often a collaborative effort as they described the occasions for the various dances that would be taught for any given class. Often the dances were commemorative in nature for special occasions like harvest time, wedding celebrations, and circumcisions. The movements carried a narrative action, like parts of speech in a syntactically-correct sentence. An example would be a palm cupped into a gourd and lifted and poured in a single motion to indicate a libation being poured onto soil. The process of learning about the cultural context, being given the name, and then learning the motions was a powerful and visceral link to a severed cultural tie experienced by African Americans during the Middle Passage of the slave trade. The transportation of slaves from the West Coast of Africa to the Americas involved a physical, psychological, and cultural loss for everyone forced to make it. Coming under this dance tutelage was like taking a step back in time to regain a lost history. While I enjoyed this exposure for its physical, psychological, and spiritual benefits, there was still a level of cultural separation involved in partaking of it on American soil. For example, I never connected the act of learning the dance to celebrate circumcision with my personal views on the practice itself.

I had first become intellectually familiar with the practice of FGM in the early 1990s, when I read Nawal El Saadawi's *Woman at Point Zero* (1975, 1983). I then read African American author Alice Walker's novel on the topic, *Possessing the Secret of Joy* (1992), in which she describes a chicken scratching up what had recently been excised from a woman's body in an FGM ritual. Ultimately, it was Somalian supermodel Waris Dirie who brought broad international attention to FGM in the late 1990s. These texts led the way for people in the West to become familiar with the practice, and they are still relevant today. It is, however, the way Sembène dares to bring to the screen the physical pain women experience during intercourse—to the point of a woman biting her own little finger until it bleeds—after the procedure that clarified in my mind his profound work on behalf of global feminism. Each frame of *Moolaadé* is composed around an underlying discourse of *I know you, I love you, but I must open your eyes to the perils of gendered traditionalism.*

Later, I contrasted the earlier perspective of my freshmen students on the topic of poor kids stealing food in Bulawayo's novel with the perspective of more seasoned undergraduates responding to Adichie's *Americanah*. My students who read Adichie's novel were much more engaged in the story and better able to relate to many of the protagonist's woes involving cultural dissonance, interracial relationships, and the complex terrain of American racism to their own middle-class experiences. While this latter set of students had read more broadly than college freshmen, the significant difference was that Adichie's novel was more accessible to them because of the middle-class politics that she presents.

Too often educators are tempted to access student empathy by presenting the saddest, most tortured and traumatic tales of Africa they can find. Of course, this strategy can backfire, because it reiterates the one-dimensional point of view most Americans already have of the African continent. The only way to achieve balance in cultural immersion is to avoid presenting stories from a single perspective without balancing it out with a second literary or filmic narrative from an alternate viewpoint.

I have never been to Africa. I have been forced to decline twice. The first time I was thwarted by a lack of funds. The second time I was due to go to Egypt when the Arab Spring took place. Despite my travel being forestalled by circumstance, I have challenged myself to learn as much as I can about life on the vast continent. I recently counted the number of African countries I have read representative literary works from. To the best of my recollection, the number of countries was twelve, with the actual works in the dozens, the majority from Nigeria. When I confessed my number to my freshmen students, they looked stricken. "You expect us to read literature from every African country?" I told them that I would be very impressed if they did, but one or two countries was a good place to start.

8

I WANT TO LIVE, AND I WANT EVERYONE ELSE TO WANT IT, TOO

You don't have the answers to everything, but this you know: mourning should never be a solitary act.

It is a winter night in early January, and I receive a phone call with devastating news: someone my child knows has committed suicide. As parents, in moments like these, you feel powerless. Still unsure of the outcome, you allow the technician in you to take over, and you pack a bag and hit the road after reserving a hotel room in the city where all of this has taken place. No one has all the answers to life's many dilemmas but this I do know: mourning should never be a solitary act.

When we arrive, my child is puffy-eyed, inconsolable, and exhausted. She is a college sophomore and her world has just received a shattering blow. My husband

and I begin to make plans, because plans are the remedy for being sideswiped in life; the mind needs to be busied in the face of death. We will go to the bridge tomorrow where her friend took his life, roses and daisies in hand, and pay homage to youth snatched from friends and family too soon. We will speak words to honor a shortened life. We will leave a memorial of sacred objects—a smiling photo of happier times, a typed statement, more bouquets of flowers—so that strangers will know that hearts were broken here. We will fulfill the rites of mourning.

Only several days before this phone call, I received another: my daughter asking whether or not she should call the police after she checked with her friend's roommates and found out he had been missing for almost forty-eight hours. She worried that he would be upset if he was just staying over at a friend's house and she put out a missing person's report on him. I immediately thought about the twenty-four-hour rule for missing persons, and the fact that the more time passed, the less likely it was that a person would be found alive. With a creeping sense of foreboding, I told her to call the police immediately. Only twenty-four hours passed between filing the missing person's report and receiving the callback from a detective that her friend, only a college freshman, was gone. Amid the fallout from this news, memories of a similar situation we'd faced nearly a decade before surfaced. My daughter must have been twelve at the time. While out driving, an emergency signal had come across our car radio. Curious, my daughter asked, "What's that sound?" I explained, "It's an emergency broadcast signal. In a few seconds they will give us details on the specific emergency." We waited and, sure enough, a mechanized voice came on and explained that there was an Amber Alert out for our area, and gave the name of the victim and the place where they were last seen. Almost immediately my daughter said, "Oh my God, Mom, I know her!" and burst into tears. I quickly went into triage mode and explained there was a good chance that she would be found. I assured her, "A family member probably picked her up, and her parents just forgot." The girl from the alert was eventually retrieved, but the circumstances of this current loss that involved a young man, a bridge, and a gun would have no happy ending.

The recent opioid crisis in America is a conversation that overlaps those based on the increased suicide rate among teens. Like opioid addiction, people are fearful of suicide reaching epidemic proportions. We live in fear of suicidal ideation and the debate over whether a popular Netflix show is promoting awareness of suicide or emulation of the act. These conversations come on the heels of news from local high schools trying to contend with multiple suicides in a single school year. What do you do when there seems to be a silent epidemic unfolding in your town? You talk. In an era when the suicide rates in small towns are paralleled by high-profile celebrity suicides like Anthony Bourdain, Kate Spade, and Kristoff St. John open communication has to be a first step to prolonging life.

As a parent, I strive to be open and honest with my kids—particularly my oldest. Every time I would come across some trending information as she was growing up, I would turn it into a teachable moment. I vividly recall when "lipstick parties" became a thing in a neighboring high-income suburban enclave. This was a phenomenon that was taking place among middle-schoolers gathering for parties where girls performed oral sex on their male counterparts. The lipstick? Well, you can figure that out. Of course, as a parent, I was horrified, but I immediately mentioned the article to my daughter, who was then in middle school, and followed up with a discussion of the many STDs that could be contracted by performing oral sex on promiscuous boys. Even if this new information only made her pause for a moment if presented with the opportunity, I figured that alone made my bringing it up worth it. The secret to this whole conversation taking place with such ease was me bringing it up like I was discussing a sale going on at The Gap or a new restaurant that just opened up in town. No judgment and no condemnation.

This is also how I learned about the pharmaceutical trade taking place on high school campuses. Adderall to focus and Ativan to mellow. It's great if you can be diagnosed with ADHD. If not, you buy on the sly. The attention to mood-stabilizing cocktails is a dedicated ritual. This is how you get through life as a teen in the 2000s. Today, mental health is managed on the down-low until you go legit with an on-call therapist and gain access to a psychiatric care plan. This is survival.

I am teaching one day when I see a student of mine nodding off in the back of the room. I have worried about her from day one. She is introverted and wears her hair big enough to obscure most of her face. She looks like she dresses in the dark and drags herself from bed fifteen minutes before each class. I want to tell her that she can shed this high school shell and reinvent herself now that she is in college. I want to take her to a salon that manages difficult hair. I know they exist; I have had difficult hair my whole life. I want to free her from the bondage of drudgery and get her excited about life. I want to see her confident face.

I invite her to my office to discuss her lack of progress in my class. After discussing and diagnosing her writing issues, she tells me that she is on psychotropic meds, but they are making her feel terrible. I gently explain that she does not have to live like this and she should call her psychiatrist immediately. I assure her that there is a medication out there that will help her deal with stress and enjoy a decent quality of life. She promises me she'll make the phone call.

I understand anxiety and stress. Many of my college students juggle two jobs, academics, extra-curricular activities and, unsurprisingly, experience high levels of stress and anxiety. Additionally, there are plenty of students who, by virtue of being first-generation college students, are now deemed capable of managing their parents' lives. These are parents who, in some cases, are themselves wrestling with drug and alcohol addiction. These same students also co-parent siblings with grandparents while being full-time students. As a final balancing act, these students also fret over the world they will inherit. They bemoan the fact that their secondary education did not prepare them for college-level critical thinking. They soon realize they existed in a bubble that was framed by Disney movies, young adult sci-fi and fantasy novels, and gaming. They were protected from discussing serious issues because their parents, teachers, and communities wanted to protect their innocence. It is devastating to be introduced to a litany of real-world problems in multiple disciplines at eighteen and told, "This is your inheritance, now what are you going to do with it?" They need this information, they want this information, and they are angry that they did not get it sooner.

Conversations about addiction, self-care, and cultural intersectionality can be cultivated in many ways. This semester I have my students reading Louise Erdrich's *LaRose* and Sherman Alexie's *You Don't Have to Say you Love Me* (2017). They are intrigued by the history of the Carlisle School that Erdrich writes about in *LaRose*. The site of the Carlisle Indian Industrial School is a little over an hour away from the college where they are now learning about the school's original mission to assimilate Native American children at the turn of the twentieth century. By the time we switch gears from fiction to memoir, they quickly marvel at Alexie's confession to being bipolar and once battling with alcoholism in a Bill Moyers interview. They are also awed by his literary production. Alexie's transparency encourages them to believe that they can make it; even brilliantly prolific people have therapists, take meds, and succeed in life.

Later that night, I get into a deep discussion with my husband about why elementary and secondary school curriculums need a major overhaul. He reminds me of one of our son's middle school teachers being raked over the coals for trying to teach the students something about Muslim culture. Parents at the school became convinced that she was trying to convert the kids instead of teaching them something about today's pluralistic America. I explain that young people are being pressed into experiencing life on too many fake planes of existence. They cannot be real in school and they cannot be real at home—there is nowhere for them to express their concerns about the world. Worst of all, they have to pretend they are happy with all of these false realities. Harkening back to a previous conversation, my husband's response is that he is not sure high schools should be teaching young kids about lynching. I chastise him for perpetuating the American tradition of undereducating to maintain childhood innocence. I remind him of the little black boy I had recently read about, who lived in New Hampshire, and was almost lynched on a playground by white high school boys who instructed him to place a rope around his own neck.

The complex interplay of traumatic history and present-day mental health on high school and college campuses is real. I am convinced that four years of college is not enough time to tell the truth about America's intricate racial, gender, and immigrant histories. A simple look at what is transpiring on our college campuses today is proof. While administrators are trying to make way for hate groups to exercise their First Amendment freedom of speech rights, their students are protesting that they deserve the right to keep their campuses safe spaces where they don't have to fear guns, hate speech, and the open threat to people of color and LGBTQ students. Students, in turn, while distrustful of administrators, will do anything to support each other.

It scares me that students are already exercising leadership to the best of their ability but getting so little help from adults behaving badly. There is a correlation between curative education, social oppression, anxiety, and drug addiction, but only one of these emerges as both component and curative.

Young adults today came of age during the Obama administration. They actually believed that a post-race society was going to be their inheritance. They knew little of the civil rights movement and Vietnam War era beyond Martin Luther King, Jr., Rosa Parks, and pot-smoking hippies. Now they wake up and check news feeds for the latest domestic terror attack, mass shooting, or climate change crisis. Young people consider heroin and oral opioids to take the edge off, and skip days of taking their anti-depressants because the medications sometimes make them feel sick or so well they feel cured.

I am not perfect; I mourn and celebrate with my students. I know that I can no more give up on them than I could on myself. Survival is not luck, it is a deliberate choice. In the words of my mother, who is over eighty now and still going strong, "You have to make up your mind early in life that you are going to be a survivor." I want nothing more than for every one of them to survive.

9

"FACING IT": OF SOLDIERS, PATRIOTISM, AND LITERARY RESISTANCE

American exceptionalism is the perception of America as a nation where any dream can become manifest based on the successful historic separation of European immigrants from their British colonial masters in 1776.

I have always been haunted by Yusef Komunyakaa's poem "Facing It," the last poem in his 1988 collection *Dien Cai Dau*. Personal loss radiates outward in the poem from the narrator's point of view along several distinct narrative threads: a confrontation with self, a depiction of a soldier's survivor's guilt, and the poignant story of a mother who kissed her boy goodbye, only to have him return home from the battlefield in a box.

My generation learned about the Vietnam War from Hollywood movies like *Apocalypse Now* (1979) and *Full*

Metal Jacket (1987), until Tim O'Brien's *The Things They Carried* (1990) became the default classroom text about the war. I visited the Vietnam War Memorial sometime after reading Komunyakaa's poem, and at that point understood just how clearly his free verse caught the play of living bodies behind names superimposed on polished granite. The title "Facing It" involves the psychic return to war that is part of the baggage that comes with memorializing a traumatic event, especially when the memorial is situated on the National Mall, the site of what to many represented the Washington, DC, power structure which guiltlessly endorsed the fighting of the Vietnam War.

I admire the way the narrator situates himself as subject in the opening lines:

> *My black face fades,*
> *hiding inside the black granite.*
> *I said I wouldn't*
> *dammit: No tears.*
> *I'm stone. I'm flesh.*

This treatment of blackness in the first two lines is seemingly passive. On the surface, the narrator makes note of the fact that his skin reflects a certain way to the play of light on polished black stone. This perspective is secondary, though, to the emotion of not seeing his name there alongside the others who didn't make it.

In a split second the narrator is forced to consider what making it really means, because despite being present, "My clouded reflection eyes me / like a bird of prey." Even as he seeks to make his peace with the war, he feels that he is still being hunted: "I go down the 58,022 names, / half-expecting to find / my own in letters like smoke."

According to the Poetry Foundation website, Komunyakaa served in the Vietnam War as a press correspondent from 1969–70. The African American soldier as subject and narrator in Komunyakaa's poem is symbolically important to me. During my formal education of American history, I always believed my own family dwelt outside the national armed forces narrative. I knew nothing of our familial legacy relative to military service. The best I could do was recall watching Sunday afternoon television with my father and his preference for old black and white World War II movies. These films rarely contained African American soldiers, so my perspective of the black soldier as narrator was nonexistent. Years later, however, I would learn that three men in my family fought in WWII. Two were my father's brothers, and one was his uncle. His uncle lost his life in the war, while one of his brothers died in a gun accident while home on furlough. Learning about these particular histories put a new spin on his interest in WWII films. I now believe he was looking for first-hand knowledge of the war to bring him closer to the soldiers who had perished in his family. Like film, literature can satisfy this need for first-hand battle tales.

The early dearth of knowledge about the military men in my family certainly made me more attuned to the black soldier's story when I encountered it in literature. The lines "I touch the name Andrew Johnson; / I see the booby trap's white flash" for me immediately recall the tragic vision of the African American soldier Shadrack and his WWI experience in Toni Morrison's novel *Sula* (1973). Morrison evokes the luck of the draw circumstances of the battlefield in three swift sentences:

> *He ran, bayonet fixed, deep in the great sweep of men flying across this field. Wincing at the pain in his foot, he turned his head a little to the right and saw the face of a soldier near him fly off. Before he could register shock, the rest of the soldier's head disappeared under the inverted soup bowl of his helmet.*

The brilliance of Morrison's writing is that her language makes readers recoil in horror equal to that of the fictional witness to such a violent death. What better logic could she have used to help civilians understand warfare than to place them in the middle of the action? Morrison drags readers deeper into the soldier's psyche by examining Shadrack's reckoning with PTSD after being wounded and before his subsequent release from a military hospital:

Like moonlight stealing under a window shade an idea
insinuated itself: his earlier desire to see his own face.
He looked for a mirror; there was none. Finally, keeping his
hands carefully behind his back he made his way to the
toilet bowl and peeped in. The water was unevenly lit by
the sun so he could make nothing out. Returning to his cot
he took the blanket and covered his head, rendering the
water dark enough to see his reflection. There in the toilet
water he saw a grave black face. A black so definite, so
unequivocal, it astonished him. He had been harboring a
skittish apprehension that he was not real.

I cannot escape Morrison's orchestration of a scene where the soldier, released from battle, must now find himself by literally locating himself in the present. Komunyakaa depicts this same need to ground oneself when his narrator observes:

I turn that way—I'm inside
the Vietnam Veterans Memorial
again, depending on the light
to make a difference.

Shedding light on the truth of existence is important, as much in real life as it is in the literary lives of Morrison and Komunyakaa's soldiers. Existence is proof of life, and warfare demands a confrontation with mortality because not everyone returns from the battle intact—psychologically or physically.

My father did not fight in the Vietnam War. Soon after receiving his draft notice, he headed to the enlistment office to request deferment. He was treated like they had never heard the word deferment before and processed like any other draftee, with a medical exam, shots, and paperwork. Ultimately, however, as a college student, husband, and father, his deployment was deferred. He reminded me that this was a war during which a lot of black men, largely from Southern states, were sent off to battle. This alarm was raised publicly by Martin Luther King, Jr., in his speech "Why I am Opposed to the War in Vietnam." In his speech, King makes the following observation:

> *We were taking the black young men who had been crippled by society and sending them 8,000 miles away to guarantee liberties in Southeast Asia which they had not found in southwest Georgia and East Harlem. So, we have been repeatedly faced with a cruel irony of watching Negro and white boys on T.V. screens as they kill and die together for a nation that has been unable to seat them together in the same schoolroom.*

Earlier in his speech, King obliquely refers to this racial inequity as an aspect of the "superficial patriotism" ignored by proponents of the war. It was an era when

Americans began to question a patriotism that raised so many ethical issues in the face of domestic hypocrisy around race equity and economic reform. Here again are the echoes of Komunyakaa's "Facing It," which elide the black face of the narrator with a white vet and grieving mother. The bullets of war did not discriminate against who they took; the grieving touched all races and genders.

Over the past few years, I have found myself using Ocean Vuong's *Night Sky With Exit Wounds* (2016), a collection which also deals with the Vietnam War, regularly in my creative writing workshops. For me, Vuong's poem "Of Thee I Sing" evokes just as much conversation about patriotism as it does American exceptionalism and immigration. We often think of American patriotism as having a monolithic ethos, but there is always a political understory. American exceptionalism is the perception of America as a nation where any dream can become manifest based on the successful historic separation of European immigrants from their British colonial masters in 1776. In the poem "Of Thee I Sing," Vuong shatters the narrative of American exceptionalism through his chronicle of the assassination of John F. Kennedy from the point of view of his wife, Jacqueline Kennedy. Vuong slows down time to highlight these connections in the post rifle shot moments of Kennedy's assassination: I'm reaching across the trunk / for a shard of your memory, / the one where we kiss & the nation / glitters."

In these precious seconds, the state of the nation is tied to a literal and figurative romanticization of the first couple as metonym for nation. In the lines "But I'm a good / citizen, surrounded by Jesus", readers are struck by the reference of allegiance to one nation tied to a mono-theistic god. Vuong also invokes the limitless vistas of the nation with its green fields and endless blue skies before delivering the poem's final blow: "My one white glove, glistening pink—with all / our American dreams." In these lines he reveals the utter desecration of a nation that continues to see itself as invincible, a nation clearly forgetting that the hallmarks of America were always improvisation and nontraditionalism, a progressive framework for change, not invincibility.

Like the limbs and bodies lost in the obdurate granite of Komunyakaa's Vietnam Veteran's Memorial, Vuong highlights the loss of national innocence in the murder of a fallen American president. The timeliness of Vuong's poem delivers in the complicated layering of his lyric, including the nature of the evil interloper revealed as the unseen catalyst of the whole event. We recognize this evil all too well. Somehow Vuong's bird's-eye view of Kennedy's assassination takes on new meaning in an era where the assassin is no longer exceptional. Historically, we have tracked his move from presidential cavalcade to Lorraine Motel balcony. When we were not looking, he entered the rural as well as the suburban high school, and even breached the university classroom.

He single-handedly created the phenomenon of the lockdown drill, institutional-wide cell phone emergency alert, and the mantra "run, hide, fight."

Yes, we bemoan the plots of national villains, actively resist the monikers new or normal. Like soldiers, we search for revelation and groundedness following unforeseen events. Our search for unity still involves a simultaneous groping to redefine patriotism. Patriotism, by definition, is a love of country: in the words of Vuong's Jacqueline Kennedy, "They have a good citizen / in me. I love my country." Like the Vietnamese American creator of this poem, a nation benefits when it embraces new ways of interpreting American history. Vuong nudges the nation to resist traditionalist values which depend on outmoded, romantic national narratives. We become spellbound. We listen and watch intently as an immigrant Vietnamese poet retells the American tale of the nation's loss of an Irish president, also the descendant of immigrants. We believe him when he intuits that the "dream" must be built on something more substantial, and know it will take every ounce of our humanity to get there.

"Facing It" is really a poem of reconciliation. It is a poem in a collection that takes readers through various iterations of war to arrive at a conclusion that involves a confrontation with the here and now. Today, when most Americans think about war, they might predictably consider the acts of domestic terrorism that have reinvigorated nationwide discussion of gun control. These tragic events have made Americans think about conflict and community in different ways. We have come to know too well the emphatic red-letter graphics of breaking news alerts that arrest us in our tracks. We know we must face the lurid details of violence until, finally, headshots flash onto our screens: the contemporary soldiers on a battlefield we never could have imagined.

10

SONNY BOY: AN ELEGY

They were just boys, Sonny Boy and Edgar. Sonny Boy was twenty-one when he died. Edgar was only nineteen when he pulled the trigger.

I remember what I wore on the day I almost shot my head off at age three: a navy-blue sweater with a red and blue plaid kilt. A thoughtful adult had arranged my hair into a half-dozen thick braids down to my shoulder blades, each one clipped with a small red plastic barrette—the type little girls still wear and that are often molded into the shape of flowers.

My near-death experience took place while I was playing with an old rifle in the sky-blue concrete storage shed, affectionately called "the little house," adjacent to my grandmother's home in central Florida. The gun was wedged between some old furniture and boxes. Unobserved, I worked quietly to pull the trigger while trying to peer down the barrel. On that fall afternoon, instead of my head being blasted to kingdom come, I walked away with a thick trickle of blood oozing from a skinned finger snagged by a rusty trigger. I also remember the fear in the eyes of the adults in my family as they gathered around me and my wounded finger. What I did not know at that time was the reason behind those fearful looks: decades before, my grandmother had lost her eldest son, Emory, to domestic gun violence. The historical subtext that was part of that moment haunted me for years to come.

My subsequent encounters with guns were also, thankfully, near misses. There was the time that my father almost picked me off after coming back from a family vacation. My parents used to take me and my three siblings on two-week long vacations to visit extended family during the summer. Upon our return, my father would go through the house with a handgun to make sure no one had taken up residence during our absence.

It was past midnight after one of these trips when my stepmother sent me into the house before my father came back out to give us the standard all-clear sign. The only item I was responsible for carrying into the house was my walk-with-me doll, Crystal; she was just my height at age eight, with the same shade of brown skin as me. Clutching her hard, plastic body tightly to my chest, I made my way down the carpeted hallway toward my bedroom. Suddenly, the figure of my father loomed in the hallway in front of me. He stood there with his legs spread and his arms outstretched before him, and at the end of his arms was a handgun pointed directly at Crystal's head. Somehow, I knew not to move or say a word. Over the play of seconds, I watched recognition slowly dawn in my father's eyes as he lowered the handgun before erupting,

"What are you doing in here? You were supposed to wait outside until I came back to get you!"

Realizing that this was now the moment to talk fast, I responded quickly. "Mommy sent us in."

I found out later that my father, so shaken by the incident, shared the news of almost shooting his oldest daughter with one of his sisters that very night.

My next gun encounter was a couple of years later. One day, my sister discovered the very same handgun at the top of my parents' closet in one of my stepmother's old purses. I recall that the inquisitive culprit gathered all four kids together with the promise of showing us a gun. The rest of us didn't believe it, of course, but proof was quickly produced when the sibling in question used a chair to reach the top of the closet and pulled down an old beige leather handbag. Reaching inside, she extracted the small black revolver. Remembering this revolver from past experience, I was afraid to touch it, even if only to take it from her and put it back into the purse. I watched another sibling reach out to weigh the gun gingerly between her small hands before I came to enough to snap "Put it back!" Regaining some authority, I told my sister to return the purse to the shelf where it had come from and not to bother it again or I would tell Mom and Dad. As I recall, it never came down again, because the next find was a diaphragm in a neat plastic case and, though we tried, we could not figure out what it was on successive tours of examination.

Looming over all three of these experiences was the specter of my grandmother's son Emory and the sketchy cautionary tale of what can happen when guns and loved ones come together. It was not, however, until the summer of 2015 that I followed up on a news trail that might lead me to further details regarding my uncle Emory White's death from a gunshot wound only a few days after his safe return from active duty in World War II. The only information I possessed to guide me was an approximate date of a shooting, and a name.

The shooting was a story that family members had referred to obliquely over the years but never fully recounted. The pact of silence around the event dealt with the fact that Emory lost his life at the hands of one of his younger brothers. The details were suppressed to assuage the guilt of the living, although by the time I encountered the news article that represented one of the few tangible records of the event, those directly involved had been dead for many years. Still, it was with a feeling of breaking a familial taboo that I held a reproduction of the newspaper article in my hands for the first time and read the scant twelve lines that revealed more of the story surrounding Emory's death than I had ever heard during my childhood.

The scant details regarding the 1946 event were nestled between the popular comic strips of the day— Donald Duck, Red Ryder, and Vic Flint—and the radio station program listings (television was still not a regular household item), which included Louella Parsons, the popular Hollywood gossip columnist, and The Lone Ranger. Alongside these historical markers was the headline: "Mulberry Negro Held After Brother's Death." The name of the deceased, my uncle Emory, was not mentioned, but the names of another uncle, Edgar Lee White, and my grandfather, Dan White, were in print.

My uncle was not called Emory by his family, but was instead known as Sonny Boy. Over the years, I had mulled over the list of three brothers who might have been responsible for Sonny Boy's accidental death. This was based on the fact that being killed by his brother was one of the few details I knew. I imagined myself as a child detective attempting to outsmart the adults around me by proving I could figure out what they had wanted to keep secret. First, I considered my own father, the youngest of the brothers, though I ultimately ruled him out because I reasoned he didn't have the years on him necessary to wield the weapon that administered the fatal shot. Next, I wondered about another uncle, a middle child, who had died of a self-inflicted gunshot wound when I was in college. Was it possible carrying the guilt of fratricide for so many years had catapulted him into depression and, subsequently, the act of taking his own life? The psychological evidence weighed high in favor of this possibility, but there was someone else who kept me from committing to that particular hypothesis. This someone else was an uncle I could only recall meeting once in my life.

Near the end of his life, at age forty-five, Edgar, also known as Brother, had largely removed himself from active involvement in the lives of other family members. I was eight at the time of his death and could only recall him as a recluse and a rumored heavy drinker, but even these details are the stuff of family lore: half-remembered statements perhaps made by an older cousin. Yet, somehow, I felt that it was his story that was intricately tied to Sonny Boy's demise, and I was right The newspaper article confirmed it.

As I worked to reconstruct historical events, I realized I could not depend on a brief news article and snippets of a tale gleaned from childhood memory to tell the complete story. I needed to hear with my adult ears a first-hand account of the events surrounding my uncle's life and sudden death. I went directly to my aunt, who is known as the family record keeper. At age eighty-six, her mind is sharper than most people a fraction of her age. Her answers to my questions were thoughtful, deliberate, and full of anecdotes that I would never have known had I not raised such specific questions about Sonny Boy's life. My aunt told the story of my grandmother Virginia sending Sonny Boy a care package all the way to Europe—full of apples, Florida oranges, and pecans—and packing the nuts loosely enough so that they would give a hint of a rattle when he held it up to his face to shake expectantly.

I pieced together the series of events that brought Sonny Boy and Edgar together that fateful night during the celebration of Sonny Boy's twenty-first birthday. In reality, the story began three years earlier when, on July 23, 1943, Sonny Boy enlisted into the United States Army at the age of eighteen. It was the middle of World War II, and the draft was in effect. As he neared the age of military maturity, he knew what his country expected of him. He enlisted and was trained at Camp Blanding, Florida, a military base still active today. Edgar enlisted two years later in 1945, also at the age of eighteen. Neither young man knew much of the world beyond Mulberry, the rural central Florida town of their birth.

Mulberry is a little over an hour's drive from Eatonville, Florida, the region where writer Zora Neale Hurston grew up and later returned to document rural African American culture and dialect. The biographical documentary on Hurston, *Jump at the Sun* (2008), contains scenes of black-and-white archival footage of African American children playing ring games outdoors in a sandy yard and men fishing alongside a lake. These images are similar to those that would have comprised the lives of blacks around the time of World War II, when Sonny Boy was growing up in a small Florida town with his mother, father, three sisters, and three brothers. I know the film's images reflected the day-to-day life of the period from flipping through old photos of my own family full of young black boys with hair cut into tight fades and girls in white pinafores. These photographic images merged in my mind with what I witnessed during family trips taken from our house in Massachusetts to Florida during the late 1970s and early '80s.

Like many residents of the region, my grandmother was an avid fisherwoman her whole life. I remember well the long, lacquered bamboo fishing poles she and my cousins favored. These poles were ideal for avoiding the presence of shoreline alligators who were the unwanted guests of any fishing trip. In Florida, we learned early that any natural or manmade body of water was gator territory. As a child, I begged to go along to fish, but was told that I was too little and might get eaten by an alligator. In Florida, this was not just a tall tale used to scare children, it was a reality. While I was not allowed to tag along, I did learn the valuable lesson that food could still be caught in the wild and used to grace a table at mealtimes.

On these visits, I also became familiar with the history of all-black towns and black communities separated from white communities by railroad tracks. These were the years of segregation, and real-estate redlining maintained the rules of racial division. Mulberry schools were still segregated in the 1940s; black students attended the J.R.E. Lee School for elementary education, named after the one-time president of the historically black Florida A&M University in Tallahassee. If black students were interested in attending high school, however, they had to travel to nearby Bartow to attend the secondary school there. Perusing an old enlistment record, I discovered that Sonny Boy could boast of having one year of high school under his belt at the time of his military enlistment, as opposed to his younger brother Edgar, who entered the war with only a grammar school education.

I imagine both Emory and Edgar were excited about heading home on furlough together during that late fall of 1946. I am sure that they could not wait to taste the sweet meat of freshwater Florida fish fried to perfection and their mother's homemade pound cake—a blesséd departure from war rations. Perhaps, as veterans of active duty, they conspired about what parts of their war experiences to share with eager family members and what they would keep to themselves. The moment I was honing in on, however, had little to do with warm nostalgia.

It is not easy to ask witnesses to a fatal shooting what they remember about the traumatic event, even if it took place almost seventy years ago. In my aunt's version of

events, she was in the backyard when she heard the gunshot and asked aloud, to no one in particular, "What was
that?" before everyone outside, including her, began to
run toward the house *en masse*. As far as the how of the
shooting, she said that Edgar was just playing around
when Sonny Boy came to the front door. He picked up
the rifle, pointed it at the door, and said jokingly, "Who
is that out there?" Sonny Boy started laughing on the
other side. Maybe saying, "Come on, man, stop playing."
Then, within the innocent interplay between two brothers, a trigger was pulled and a bullet released. Her final
shared detail was that it had been a head wound.

The newspaper article, my touchstone, also told me
that Sonny Boy had immediately been taken to the hospital, where he died soon after arriving. He was taken
to Polk General Hospital, also known by locals as the
county hospital. The facility was originally opened in
1926 to service blacks and poor whites, and officially
closed in the 1970s. When it opened, the staff consisted of one doctor and five nurses, one of which was
African American.

The Polk General Hospital, aka county hospital,
was just under ten miles from my grandmother's home.
For the person driving that night after the shooting, those
miles must have felt interminable. The staffing during
the war years, almost two decades after opening, was
still slim because of the draft, with only one full-time and
one part-time doctor. Oddly enough, a colored hospital

was constructed on the same site in 1929. I wondered if the second hospital indicated that the original vision of a fully-integrated Polk General Hospital had fallen by the wayside only three years after construction. Was this an important detail or just a distraction from the reality that Sonny Boy had suffered a mortal head wound? With this being the case, no building or available hands could have saved him—neither in the now-white county hospital nor the colored annex that might still have been in use.

After organizing the particulars of Sonny's death, I shared my information with my father. The pause after I finished recounting the events as I believed they unfolded was long and full, but full of what I did not initially know. Finally, on an expelled breath, he said, "Wow. Thank you so much for bringing out something that had been in the dark for so long." By "in the dark," he was referring to the fact that growing up he was told he had been a baby when Sonny Boy died. Interpreting this as the literal truth, my father always believed he was two or three years old when his brother Sonny Boy was killed. The news article, however, confirmed that my father was actually eight years old. Yet, because the story was always retold as oral history like events in a play, his role was always that of the baby: the ignorant child figure without knowledge of details surrounding the actual event. Family roles have a way of stretching into adulthood. The baby of the family never learned the full story, even after raising children of his own. On this day, however, I came bearing details.

My father and I must have talked for an hour about his brother and the night he was killed. He remembered standing in front of the radio in my grandmother's living room that night, listening to music. He was dancing in the corner by himself because he was too young to drink or play cards with the older crowd. I could hear the joy in his voice as he reclaimed this private memory from his childhood, a memory lost to him for so many years. Quickly, though, he realized that he recalled the moment so vividly because it was followed by screaming and the silencing of the music by frenzied adults swarming around him after the fatal shot was fired.

Often tragic stories are put on a shelf, ostensibly to protect the psyches of the young and the living. I carried the compulsion to know this story for decades. Somewhere along the line, the compulsion morphed into a desire to tell a story bigger than bits of childhood memory and the November 17, 1946, page 7 section B headline in the *Lakeland Ledger* that read, "Mulberry Negro Held After Brother's Death."

They were just boys, Sonny Boy and Edgar. Sonny Boy was twenty-one when he died. Edgar was only nineteen when he pulled the trigger. Though he was arrested immediately after the shooting, Edgar was not charged for what was, essentially, a horrific accident. Sonny Boy and Edgar were both soldiers in a war that took them across an ocean far from Polk County, Florida, and the rural hamlet that they called home. Sadly, only one brother, Edgar, would return to Europe to safely finish out his post-war tour of duty. Unlike many soldiers who fought in World War II, they made it back home before their lives were changed forever.

11

HARD-HEADED IKE: A PAEAN TO BLACK BOYHOOD

There is a particular self-loathing that comes from not being able to assess the history and economic circumstances that led to your disadvantaged condition. This is the plight of many black men.

I am no expert on little black boys. One of my earliest memories of my relationship with my younger brother is of me organizing his Garanimals outfits in his bedroom closet. Garanimals required that you match the tags to tell which pants went with which shirts. I tried to confound the tags and match outfits randomly to see if they were still wearable; he didn't complain much.

My brother's most distinguishable feature was a large, curly afro that he twirled into thick ringlets as he slept while sucking his index finger. Around age five, he entered what my parents referred to as his "destructive phase." Suddenly, it was impossible to find a #2 pencil in the house with an intact eraser. Somehow, unobserved, my brother acquired the habit of chewing off erasers. Next, all of his toys started turning up broken. The most memorable breakage was the demise of his yellow Tonka dump truck. Tonkas were supposed to be indestructible and made for even the roughest play—not so. This was also around the time that I first heard him referred to by my parents as a hard-headed Ike. The rest of us kids didn't know who Ike was, but apparently he liked to chew off erasers and break toys—behavior that required a hard head.

Among these recollections is a more vivid, pre-destructive phase memory of my brother dressed as a cowboy with a red cowboy hat, a tooled leather belt draped around his narrow hips, and a faux ivory-handled Colt 45 in his holster. He loved this outfit, and the click of the gun's metal hammer striking the end of the barrel following the trigger pull could be heard throughout the house. Yet, how can I not think about the response that gun would get on the street today following an event like the 2014 police killing of twelve-year-old Tamir Rice for just such simple play? No one can say exactly when the cuteness factor of little black boys morphs into their being seen as armed killers, but the shift in perception has deadly consequences.

Viewed from another perspective, an intellectually disarmed black man is only a danger to himself. There is a particular self-loathing that comes from not being able to assess the history and economic circumstances that led to your disadvantaged condition. This is the plight of many black men. Over the years, I have heard too many mothers discuss the interventions they have staged on behalf of their black sons within the public school system because their child's behavior was considered disruptive. So often what would be considered acceptable behavior is deemed unsuitable for a boy if he is a child of color.

In her memoir *This Fragile Life: A Mother's Story of a Bipolar Son* (2012), author Charlotte Pierce-Baker, a fellow scholar and the wife of Houston Baker, chronicles her son's battle with mental illness, while also touching on many of the vulnerabilities black males face. In particular, she relates a story of her son's kindergarten years, when a teacher referred to him as disruptive and then divulged why:

> *In her opinion, Mark had been privileged in his learning, and he set the bar too high for the classroom. Her solution was to have Mark sit quietly in the corner, and he did so repeatedly, a signal to the other children that he had misbehaved. I was furious at her silencing of our son.*

I find Pierce-Baker's recollection of advocating on behalf of her son interesting in this context because he was disciplined for displaying leadership qualities. Even when young boys of color do not fit a stereotype of unpreparedness, they are still corralled according to that predictive behavior and rendered invisible.

Successful parental educational interventions ensure that young men of color beat the odds and actually make it into the classrooms of liberal arts colleges and universities around the country. Typically, when these young men have crossed my path, they have not read a book penned by an African American, nor do they have a sense of an African American intellectual tradition. In fact, the literary production that could serve to save their lives has never been discussed within their earshot. What they have learned is how not to appear threatening—a perception that could get them excused from the classroom and the institution. This is also an approach to higher education that I read as going through the motions of receiving an education without experiencing active learning.

I have come across young black men in an unwanted state of intellectual stasis throughout my academic career. On these occasions, I was always glad that I had placed on the syllabus black male voices as disparate as Langston Hughes's *The Big Sea* (1940) and James Baldwin's *The Fire Next Time* (1963), to poet Cornelius Eady's *Brutal Imagination* (2001) and poet Frank X. Walker's *Turn Me Loose: The Unghosting of Medgar Evers*. (2013). Hughes and Baldwin provide students with a black male literary genealogy from the Harlem Renaissance to the American Civil Rights era. Eady and Walker bring conversation current by elaborating on the historical record of black civil rights and contemporary media depictions of African American males. These books bring all students, regardless of their race, up to speed on a black male intellectual tradition. Additionally, they allow black men access to a racial discourse they have lived out in American society but have never been privy to in the classroom.

I recently came into contact with an African American male student suffering from intellectual malaise in one of my American literature survey courses. The class was at midterm, and nothing had touched this student all semester. His attention was lackluster and his writing equally so. He was on a steady course to receive a D in the class. He was also the first in his family to attend college. I imagined that his parents had worked hard to keep him off the streets and away from social snares that could have easily made him a homicide victim or prison statistic. Surely, I thought, there was some work in the repertoire of American literature that could arouse his intellectual curiosity. Then I introduced him to W.E.B. Du Bois's *The Souls of Black Folk* and watched his whole classroom demeanor undergo a sea change; it was like Du Bois himself had entered the room and shaken this student to his core.

The Du Boisian spell was cast when my student read the essay "Of the Training of Black Men." He was fascinated by the fact that, at the turn of the twentieth century, someone was dedicated to advocating a liberal arts education for black men. In Du Bois's time, this incredible goal was voiced too few years after the emancipation of slavery and during an era of frequent lynchings of black people across the South. Suddenly, this student realized that he was the beneficiary of generations of black educators invested in black men during periods of rampant racial violence against the black body. Du Bois was teaching in the South when black men were still being hung from trees, driven out of town, and run off their farms because they were seen as a threat to an established racial hierarchy. This hierarchy demanded that they remain at the bottom of a Southern caste system that required they appear to be less enfranchised than impoverished whites. My student made the imaginative leap through time and saw his own potential amid the current backdrop of dire US statistics for African American economic progress. Today, the same racial hierarchy is maintained through black and brown incarceration and educational marginalization. In retaliation, my student chose to change his statistical outlook.

I was introduced to the legacy of W.E.B. Du Bois while studying journalism as an undergraduate at the University of Massachusetts, Amherst, when one of my professors sent me out to interview possibly the only black instructional journalist then on campus: David Graham Du Bois. Graham Du Bois was the stepson of W.E.B. Du Bois via his marriage to Shirley Graham. While an avid reader of James Baldwin and Maya Angelou as a child growing up in Massachusetts, I had not read W.E.B. Du Bois. I do, however, remember how sensitive his stepson was about my naivety. He answered all of my questions after first arming me with a mini-lecture on his stepfather. He then moved on to the basics, including the pronunciation of the famous name and his preference for the American version over the French. The white male professor who directed me David's way did me a good turn by planting a seed that day. Years later, I would read Du Bois thoroughly as a graduate student and make a point of mentioning his name in nearly every course I taught thereafter. Works that left a deep impression included *The Souls of Black Folk* (1903), *Black Reconstruction* (1935), and *Darkwater* (1920). In 1896, Du Bois was the first African American to graduate from Harvard University with a PhD. He anchored the twentieth-century African American intellectual tradition and remains the most erudite African American theorist who ever lived. Without his legacy, no others could have followed in his footsteps.

Telling a story and telling the right story are two distinct actions, the greater value definitely lying in the latter. I am always looking for stories that describe the present-day hurdles that young black men face and manage to overcome. All to the better if these stories offer historical insight into institutional racism. Martha Southgate's *The Fall of Rome* (2002) is one of those stories that gives you a lot of bang for your pedagogical buck. It is a rags-to-intellectual-riches tale of two African American brothers who have the chance to attend an elite Massachusetts private school on scholarship. One brother inadvertently falls prey to the very streets he is trying to escape, while the other must work hard to change the institution that claims to want to help him. The book addresses an array of themes: black masculinity, engaged black parenting, racial micro-aggressions, urban violence, the history of the Great Migration, the history of the Black Power movement, parental grief, white allies, classism, educational elitism, and institutional racism. It is an instructional goldmine.

Though this should go without saying, black books are not just for black young adults. Everyone stands to gain from reading the stories of young black men, and I affirmed this theory when I recently introduced my two white stepsons to Southgate's novel. Our older son is an avid cross-country runner, a sport that the protagonist of the novel is introduced to when he begins to attend a private boys school. Predictably my older stepson, who attended private school, identified with the setting and the way the sport was discussed in the novel, and found it a good read. My younger stepson said it was one of the best books he had ever read and definitely better than anything he had encountered in his public school education up to that point as a high school freshman. When I asked why, he said he could identify with the protagonist, an African American teen. Upon further discussion, I found what he really connected with was the contemporary time period and race-engaged dialogue" that frame the novel's plot development. Coupled with that, the novel served to fill the gaps of what he often heard snippets of on televised news reports. The novel's protagonist loses his brother to gun violence while he is walking to a bodega for a Coke; my stepson, in turn, was not unaware of Tamir Rice's death while playing on the street in the neighborhood where he lived. While my stepson had not had these experiences of personal loss through gun violence, he could still identify with the teenage struggle with life issues that pervade the novel.

I thought back on this conversation with my younger stepson when he recently told me that he was looking forward to a cross-country trip to the Smokies. Like his older brother, he is also an enthusiastic member of his high school cross-country team. However now, with a slightly aggravated tone, he mentioned that some of the team members had decided that one of their themed running days would be "Redneck" day. According to him, "I think it's stupid, and I am just going to run in my regular clothes." I agreed with his assessment. He then went on to say that a couple of the guys on the team were African American. I asked if he thought that they were comfortable with "Redneck" day being the theme for the run, and he said no. I then asked if he cared about their feelings, and he admitted that he did. I then explained that people often interpret silence as agreement, and if he felt that the term had racial implications for his team-mates, he should speak up about it.

My stepson's dilemma did not surprise me. Our older daughter had attended the same Tennessee high school at a time when students wanted to have a "Redneck"–themed day leading up to commencement, and on that occasion students had spoken out in protest.

The urban dictionary defines a "Redneck" in various ways, but the most damaging defining terms are some-one who lives in a rural community in the South and is xenophobic while harboring deep racist sentiments—the very qualities that are currently pulling apart our nation in the twenty-first century. This level of cultural traditionalism in the guise of team and school spirit obvi-ously disrespects racial difference and reinforces racial bias on a fundamental level.

There is no doubt in my mind that my stepson came to consciousness when he read Southgate's book. Too often coming to racial consciousness is seen as a rite of passage for African American kids and the chil-dren of people of color at large. My stepson's concern and feelings of empathy for his African American male teammates in response to "Redneck" day is an example of good character we should all expect from our children as they are confronted with various forms of racial bias.

Somewhere along the line, I started to have conver-sations with my white stepson that I would have had with a black son. Sometimes the conversations took longer, because I needed to add a lot of historical context that he did not naturally experience as a white male moving through society, but he paid close attention.

Like during the revelation our family experienced on a recent trip to the Baltimore Museum of Art in Maryland. After viewing the museum exhibit, we headed outside to find a bare concrete foundation where a statue of Robert E. Lee and Stonewall Jackson had once stood. After a few minutes, I recalled that Baltimore Mayor Catherine Pugh had removed it during the heated summer of 2017 because it was "in the best interest of my city," days after the Charlottesville protest in Virginia had resulted in violence and the loss of several lives (*New York Times*, Aug. 2017). Walking around the concrete base where the statues once stood, I was chilled by the fact that the words chiseled there still advocated for the will of the Confederacy to provoke national disunity: "So great is my confidence in General Lee that I am willing to follow him blindfolded. Straight as the needle to the pole Jackson advanced to the execution of my purpose." The "purpose" invoked in this line was to overcome the Union Army and the will of America to remain one nation.

Part of the American racial disconnect in the public school system, elementary through secondary and beyond, is that students encounter no credible discourse on systemic racism in the United States. In many school curriculums, race is discussed as if the American Civil

Rights movement and resultant civil rights-era legislation set all racial inequity straight once and for all. The consequence is that books like *To Kill A Mockingbird* and autobiographical details about the lives of Martin Luther King, Jr. and Rosa Parks are the end of the national discourse. It leads students to believe that the work of national racial division was handled by their parents or grandparents' generation, and America has largely overcome its racially charged history. Even when the American Civil Rights movement is discussed, it is done so selectively, often omitting the most revealing of historic racial hate crimes.

The 1955 murder of fourteen-year-old Emmett Till galvanized a nation and served as a catalyst for a prolonged and dedicated examination of African American civil rights. Till was murdered by white men because he reputedly whistled at a white woman. I think about the enduring injustice of Till's murder as the news reports the July 2019 emergence of a photograph of University of Mississippi students posing with automatic weapons in front of the bullet-ridden sign commemorating the site where his mutilated and murdered body was found. The commemorative sign has been vandalized and replaced on repeated occasions over the years, proving that many still believe his death was justified. For me, the photograph is just more evidence of what happens when history is not contextualized by secondary school or university educators with social justice training.

The manufactured tableau of current college students with guns in front of the bullet-riddled sign commemorating the death of a murdered 14-year-old indicate that these young white men identify more with Till's murderers than they do with Till—a boy only a few years younger than them.

One might wonder how this error in institutional policy regarding diversity training and diversity literature affects post-secondary classroom instruction. Not long ago, a black mother told me how a white professor's use of the n-word in class served to shut down her daughter's performance in class and eventually garnered her child a failing grade for the course, because she was no longer interested in performing for a teacher whom she could not respect. To be clear, the professor used the n-word after first letting a hip hop song do it for her. She then used the song as a segue into a discussion of whether or not use of the n-word was appropriate in black music. Apparently, during the discussion, both white and black students freely and repeatedly used the actual word instead of the safe-space reference "n-word" as the appropriate classroom term. My friend's daughter was traumatized by her peers as well as the educator whose care she was under in the classroom.

I was not surprised by the outcome of this situation. In their zeal to be "hip" and "down," professors are frequently careless about thinking through how to talk about race, language, and subjectivity in the classroom. Rather than using several essays by different African American critics to discuss the issues, they often choose other mediums of popular culture and attempt to perform an impromptu critique based on their own limited knowledge base. No, listening to hip hop alone does not make you a cultural critic. While this professor went on to collect her paycheck, at least one student suffered psychological trauma from her careless pedagogy. Additionally, while the numbers may not be readily available, plenty of students of color do leave academic institutions because they feel unsupported in the classroom resulting from similar classroom displays. I myself dropped a class as a graduate student at NYU on the first day of class when a professor started off his first lecture with the words "gay people are the new n-word." Needless to say, he used the actual word, not the shorthand. I looked around, saw that I was the only black person in the class, and walked out without looking back. I'm sure he is somewhere still reveling in his self-proclaimed brilliance.

Intellectual gatekeeping is real. Success is not genetically ordained; it is cultivated. Telling the right story at the right time is one way to open the door for everyone.

12

BURGER PRINCESS: ON THE BUSINESS OF BEING UPPER-MIDDLE CLASS AND BLACK

According to family lore, we were the second African American family to live in Wilbraham. Then the unthinkable happened; the first black pioneers moved out and we became the only black family in town.

As a child of the '80s, I fondly remember Springfield, Massachusetts, as the site of my first concert: Parliament Funkadelic, where one of the band members conspicuously sported a diaper onstage and I wore my first spaghetti-strap dress. The slinky blue-green fabric clinging to my youthful curves almost made anyone who saw me forget the gold teardrop eyeglass frames, replete with coke-bottle thick lenses, reverse-magnifying my large eyes to doll-sized ones. Despite this, when the group asked "Do you promise the funk, the whole funk, nothin' but the funk?", I shouted my promise like the multitudes around me, proving it by standing for three straight hours in four-inch cork wedges.

It was the Burger King Corporation that rolled out the red carpet bringing us to Springfield, Massachusetts. A decade following President Lyndon B. Johnson's passing of the Civil Rights Act that opened up fair business opportunities for African Americans, the company welcomed enterprising blacks interested in becoming restaurant franchisees. Deal sealed, my parents packed our goods into a Mayflower moving truck in Miami, Florida, and headed up I-95, eventually meeting up with the jaunty Pilgrim hat signs guiding us along I-90, the Massachusetts Turnpike.

Today, I can mention the name of the town we lived in, the Springfield suburb of Wilbraham, to anyone who lives in the Northeast, and they will recognize it as the home of Friendly's Ice Cream; the tell-tale script-lettered hedge on the interstate still testifies to the fact. Historically, the town was founded on tragedy. In the mid-eighteenth century, a young boy named Timothy Merrick, from the then-village of Wilbraham, was killed by a rattlesnake on a local mountaintop. I assume this settler footnote was meant to show how important children were to the town even during its pioneer years. Despite its somewhat isolated locale, growing up I found much to appreciate in this rural hamlet.

Our home in western Massachusetts was situated

within a woodsy enclave. Just behind our house were plentiful blueberry bushes where an occasional deer plucked delicately at the tasty berries. Heading deeper into the woods, one could easily spot patches of wild raspberries. Beyond the snackable wildlife, the warren of trails at our back door were extensive and great for biking and walking. Other than encountering the occasional battered copy of *Playboy* or *Hustler* on a trail—no doubt abandoned by a group of teens—these woods were a bucolic haven. Looking back, I see my forays into the woods as a safety net from the social pressures of being a minority in small-town America.

According to family lore, we were the second African American family to live in Wilbraham. Then the unthinkable happened; the first black pioneers moved out and we became the only black family in town. What did this mean? Well, we basically became anomalies waiting for other anomalies to move to town so we would not stand out as much as we did. During our time in this humble colonial town, several other black families moved in, and we befriended the kids from at least two of them. One family consisted of Jamaican immigrants, and the other was a military family. While my family certainly stood out because of our race, we also gained some notoriety for owning a Burger King, which made everyone who knew about it figure that we must be rich.

The day we officially opened our Burger King may or may not have been the same day memorialized in a photograph of the official ribbon-cutting. As I recall, my siblings and I spent the day running and playing under and around the brown-and-orange plastic banquet tables. When we took breaks from our energetic play, we ordered drinks and food from the skeleton crew on hand to operate the kitchen stations. I drank a lot of strawberry and chocolate milkshakes that day, and ate way too many cheeseburgers. I liked fast food as much as the next kid, but owning a Burger King did not make my parents culinary brutes. As a rule, we only officially ate fast food one day a week, so our dietary lives did not change significantly. What did change was how people related to us after they found out what my parents did for a living, especially in the city where they worked.

In Springfield, a city with a more significant black and brown population than Wilbraham, my parents became community leaders. People in the Springfield metropolitan area were glad to see a young black couple emerging as successful entrepreneurs. Everyone wanted to work for us and, if they couldn't, they definitely wanted to spend their discretionary income on our burgers to make sure we stayed in business. My parents were regularly listed as sponsors for local events. They were active in civic and social organizations like the Urban League and Jack and Jill. This meant that at least several times a year we would see them resplendent in black-tie with my stepmother running out the door still blowing on her freshly manicured nails while shouting last-minute instructions to our sitters. In this climate of determined bourgeois bliss, the ultimate "we made it" moment occurred when my father appeared in a cover story for *Black Enterprise* magazine tied to a story on the top black restaurant franchisees in the region.

In turn, my parents made sure that they supported other black businesses. When it was time to get our hair done, we traveled forty-five minutes to Hartford, Connecticut, so we could have our coifs perfected at Soul Scissors—the premier black hair salon of the moment. With four heads to contend with, it was a multi-hour event, but time well spent. To round out our urban cultural immersion experience, my stepmother also made sure that we took dance and modeling classes at the Dunbar Community Center, under the direction of Springfield's own Frank Hatchett. Hatchett would become a major jazz dance force on Broadway, going on to work with such notable entertainers as Gregory Hines, but his humble beginnings were in Springfield, Massachusetts, where he was celebrated as a favored son. I studied with him as a kid and knew him as the master teacher who came to review student progress at the end of each class.

My siblings and I were not scrappy kids, so we were regularly intimidated by our inner-city counterparts. Our daily lives were spent in Wilbraham, our predominately white hometown. In Wilbraham, classical ballet was the dance of choice. In fact, my regular ballet teacher, Mrs. Johnson, was by her own admission a one-time dancer with the Ballets Russes: the early twentieth-century dance company that launched the career of Vaslav Nijinsky. I appreciated her historical pedigree, but by the time I studied with her, she was well into her eighties with paper-thin skin and knuckled feet that looked uncomfortable in her pink ballet slippers. Despite her years, Mrs. Johnson directed her classes with an imposing demeanor, tapping her cane on the wooden floor of the grange hall while demonstrating steps through the lithe young body of her assistant, a local advanced ballet student.

In contrast, our classes at the Dunbar Center were meant to bring us closer to our African American heritage, so we didn't grow up to be like those awkward black kids who acted self-conscious around other black people. During Hatchett's more jazz-influenced version of ballet class at the Dunbar, I learned how to negotiate my way around other black girls, hands on hips, watching me with skeptical side-eye.

Both of my parents had emerged from towns where black business people often made their living from owning corner stores, barber shops, and hair salons. They loved the fact that their new fast-food business was in a diverse community where they could make a difference in the lives of the residents. The hourly employees included a healthy mix of African American, Dominican, Puerto Rican, and white workers. Located on one of the busiest corners of State Street, a major thoroughfare in the community, the Burger King catered to three local high schools—Classical, Central, and Commerce— and nearby businesses like Milton Bradley and Digital Computers. The lunch rush was an income-sustaining madhouse.

At this time, Springfield was not a site of broad economic growth. Like most cities, it had its share of homeless. On several occasions, I spied my parents donating burgers (considered expired because they had been in the bin for ten minutes and were therefore unsellable) to homeless men who came knocking at the back door. Springfield was also home to a healthy number of black churches. As Southerners who had migrated to the Northeast, my parents had been raised in the more charismatic environs of the black Baptist and African Methodist Episcopal churches. Occasionally, as a family, we would make the thirty-minute trek to the city to attend one of these churches that echoed the traditions they were raised in, but, as a matter of practicality, we more often attended the white Methodist church closer to home. In the Methodist church, we learned to sing standard hymns in a non-demonstrative manner and to hold our clapping following the performance of these hymns for another time and place. A major cultural breakthrough came when, at some point during my high school years, we acquired an African American assistant pastor at the Methodist church we attended in our small town. He became the youth pastor and took over organizing all of the young adult activities for the church. The year we gained our black youth director was also the year we attended our first retreat at Camp Atwater.

Camp Atwater, located in Brookfield, Massachusetts, is a historically black camp established in the early twentieth century to cater to the children of middle-class black families. It was created during a time when black and white kids did not regularly attend camps together: the reason behind the existence of most historically black institutions.

Attending a predominantly white school in a community in the Northeast was to experience life as a racial pioneer. School administrators and faculty were ignorant of what my siblings and I were experiencing as racial outsiders. Most of them had been groomed in homogeneous environments themselves, and did not have the experiential or intellectual tools to make our lives easier. Despite this circumstance, books became my lifeline. I read voraciously both in and out of school. In fact, books became my literal shield from the steps of the yellow school bus to the school's front door. I actually walked with my nose buried in the pages of whatever novel I happened to be reading at the time to avoid verbal pelting from racial epithets. Even under excruciating duress, kids are resilient. Amid the racial bullying, I still strove for normalcy through friendships with those brave white students willing to risk their own well-being by entering the dangerous sphere of my marginalized status. I also became friends with Jewish students and recent immigrants of multiple races.

Without a doubt, parents will go to great lengths to give their children access to the economic power center. Often these lengths include living in communities with highly-rated school systems in largely white communities. In order to live out their economic dreams, people of color must be acculturated to code-switching alongside kids weaned on country club memberships, European vacations, private school educations, and Ivy League destinies. This is the price for ensuring that children of color will not be intimidated in the face of privilege in the corporate boardroom or the academic classroom. This is the choice my parents made, and the same that I made for my own children. For many POC, this is the price of economic survival.

The last time I visited Springfield was when I traveled there with my college roommate. Burger King was her favorite fast food eatery, and she was overjoyed that we could visit my parents' restaurant and have a free, all-you-can-eat meal there. With appetites in hand, we made the forty-minute drive from Amherst to Springfield. At this point, the business had expanded to include a downtown franchise, and I remember we hit that one because my dad was monitoring the lunch rush. After our meal of Whoppers, fries, and shakes, my roommate beamed and gushed her delight all the way back to our bleak, cinder-block dorm. Not too many years after this visit, the Burger Kings would be sold and my family's foray into successful entrepreneurship would come to an end. When I think about it, anyone who walked into our house in those days could tell what kind of people we were by looking at the magazines on our freshly dusted coffee table, consisting of *Ebony*, *Jet*, *Black Enterprise*, *Essence*, *Connoisseur*, and *The Robb Report*.

13

BE READY: TALES OF RACIAL AMBUSHING IN THE ACADEMY

The clamor of white nationalism has dangerously occluded a very real history of productive interracial alliances at work in America for generations.

Growing up in Massachusetts, I was never one to have the quick comeback when I was confronted with a racial slur. When I heard a yelled "spearchucker" or "jigaboo," my heart would leap in my chest and my lips would compress, no sound of retaliation having any chance of leaving my mouth. The "f*#k you!" that would have been appropriate was language that was forbidden in our household. So I suffered in silence, only to later imagine all that I could have said to verbally slay my attacker and leave them a whimpering shell of a human being.

As an African American educator, now many years

beyond these childhood trials, I still experience bigotry within the academy. These telling revelatory moments, too, remain as fresh as an open wound. My experiential anecdotes include the tenured professor who once attacked me for being a racist when, as pre-tenure faculty, I suggested that my college invite an African American to campus as a guest speaker for the upcoming annual Martin Luther King, Jr. lecture. I was completely taken aback because, typically, this is the one occasion when one would expect minimum conflict around recommending a diverse speaker. Wrong. Not only was I called a racist, I was later waylaid by the same faculty member in the parking lot. From his pickup truck through a rolled down window, he tried to explain to me that he was not being a racist by calling me a racist, because he was colorblind and did not see race.

Believing the incident over, I was unexpectedly treated to the regular appearance of this same faculty member at my local gym, where he tried to force me to greet him every time our paths crossed before or after a workout. This simple act had the effect of reminding me of his original accusation against me on regular basis. If you are reading this situation as passive-aggressive harassment that transported me into a cycle of post-traumatic race disorder, you are correct.

Bigots do not always wear their politics openly. This is true in the same way that when someone commits a high-profile crime, people often say they never would have expected the act to come from such a kind neighbor, relative, or polite stranger. As a case in point, while I was being harassed by the previously mentioned colleague, others readily called him friend.

Sadly, I have also found that there is often no forewarning of exactly when someone is going to "act out" in a racially hostile manner. On another occasion, I had a student come to me after a class session to inform me that one of the students from the class had been working to rally others to stage a walk-out of my class because I was, in his words, "teaching racist black rhetoric." At the time, we were reading Michelle Alexander's *The New Jim Crow*. In general, the students found it informative and sound reading to better understand the institutional racism inherent in the American judicial system. Yet, before my student informer even identified the student who had tried to stage the coup, I knew to whom she was referring.

People of color learn early how to be observant of their surroundings. I had noticed this student on the first day of class, because he sported a Confederate flag decal stitched to his backpack. Additionally, he'd already confronted me in class by disagreeing with Alexander's examples of racial bias at every opportunity during class discussions. While my experience made it easy to shut him down diplomatically in the classroom, I was sure he would not pass up an opportunity to turn students to his point of view outside of my earshot. Sure enough, the student identified this same young man as the culprit. She went on to voice her concern for me and members of the class. She was alarmed by the level of his suppressed rage. She confided that other students had also been extremely uncomfortable with his hallway diatribe against me.

I am careful to maintain my classroom as a safe space for myself and my students. I did not hesitate to immediately follow procedures to track down the student and prevent him from returning to class until I could assess his intentions regarding me and the course. This is the reality of teaching about social justice issues in the twenty-first century.

Being sideswiped by racist outbursts is the old normal. I recently attended a college function to celebrate the advent of the winter holiday season. The final performer, a faculty member, proceeded to regale the audience with a piece about growing up in the South, replete with references to his father dressing up in blackface and "Negroes" all around, especially his beloved Mammy. This whole dismal spectacle was accompanied by bouncy minstrel music he played with enthusiasm as he flung the pages of recitation behind him upon finishing each one while continuing to play. The entire performance was offensive, doubly so because of the students in attendance. It was carried out with deliberate malicious intent to denigrate African Americans in a public forum in the guise of entertainment. This individual had a track record, and I felt thoroughly dehumanized by the encounter.

Students are, more often than not, the ones who assume the higher moral ground in a situation like this. That night and through the next day, I received emails from students apologizing for the outrageous performance and stating their intent to go to the administration so that the professor in question would face some kind of disciplinary action.

To show the vastly different response of faculty to the situation, I offer the following conversation that took place less than 24 hours later with a colleague:

Colleague: May I apologize for Monday night's performance on behalf of my colleague?

Me: Well, actually, I am truly shocked by the display and by the number of people who have come forward to say that this was not the first time they have been subjected to his behavior. In fact, I am surprised that someone like that has been allowed to repeatedly traumatize faculty.

Colleague: Well, that's true. That's just "Tom."

Me: Truthfully, faculty should not be expected to function in such a climate, and I see it as a failure of the institution to handle the matter.

Colleague: Yes, true. It was really quite sick.

First, I found it completely useless to apologize for someone else's actions. That is a meaningless gesture that only assuages the guilt of the person apologizing because they didn't do anything in the moment when they witnessed the affront firsthand. Also, I will add here that the apology came with a broad smile and a chuckle, as if to say "We both know that it was ridiculous, but what can we do?" There was no sense of gravitas about the situation until I used stern language to indict institutional values that allowed this person's behavior to remain unchecked. After I revealed that I was not going to accept a false apology, the "Well, that's just Tom, you know" excuse quickly fell by the wayside.

Perhaps the most eye-opening aspect of these experiences is that, like those once ill-equipped teachers of my childhood who did not understand the racism I faced in middle and high school on a regular basis, my white colleagues are often slow to react to racist behavior. They assume that any person of color who has been in the academy for at least a decade has built up enough armor that open displays of racism just pass over us like water. This is not the case. In fact, I fear for students of color in the classes of these unsympathetic faculty because of their inability to exercise empathy beyond the terrain of their own racial subject positions. If they cannot display compassion for a colleague, how would they ever be able to mediate for a vulnerable student?

This question becomes even more significant in an economy where students are often making the choice to attend state universities, and small liberal arts colleges find themselves scrambling for customers.

Inevitably, this scramble leads to targeted marketing geared toward African American students, other students of color, and economically marginalized white students. Not only are these communities brought together in a haphazard manner, they are also often left to tackle the racial cultural divide on their own. The predictable outcome of the situation is that students often self-segregate and professors continue to err by not addressing their cultural needs because they are ill-equipped, as a consequence of their own biases, to meet them.

In today's racial economy, empathy is often viewed as weakness. There is a prevailing belief that the oppressed deserve their oppression, because they have not risen enough beyond their low circumstances to thrive. A more mundane example of this social hubris can be found in the act of naming. To care about something as seemingly simple as the term by which a particular racial group prefers to be called is likened to federal-level control over nomenclature and considered an infringement upon free speech. European colonialism set the bar high for calling various world cultures out of their self-appointed names. The act of European renaming established a hierarchy that prevails to the current moment; the powerful name and the subjugated are named. The price of members of a particular race or ethnicity trying to change their name through self-empowerment is to render themselves invisible to the status quo. The refusal to deal with the issue of naming is one rationale educators use to omit referencing diverse literatures or theoretical voices in their classrooms. It boggles the mind to think that tracing the etymological shift from Negro, to colored, to black, to African American, is beyond people with several degrees behind their names. Ditto for Oriental, to Asian, to Chinese American, Korean American, or Japanese American. This circumstance makes me wonder what horrors are occurring behind closed doors against students of color and revisited on me, a professor of color, in the open.

I am sometimes made privy to these war stories in private. There was the case of the young woman who recounted her experience with an older professor who referred to her as "the colored girl" in 2016 to another student while in her earshot. She struggled with herself about correcting the professor and then wondered what she would say. The cultural demands of respecting her elders and trying to educate a senior citizen warred within her. She decided to take one for the team and not say anything, but clearly she was left with the traumatic residue. She could not remain silent in front of someone she felt could empathize with her plight, which in this case happened to be me. Her professor's careless use of outmoded racial terminology took her back in time to a historical period governed by "white only" and "colored" signs which defined where blacks could and could not go. The use of the term indicated to her that her professor still thought her body was only marginally tolerable in her classroom. This student's experience is not uncommon.

People of color must often bear the burden and stress of American race history in their daily lives. I have experienced this truth played out even in my own family life. My husband has done a great job of compiling a library of diverse literary voices for our younger, mixed-race daughter. The list prioritizes African American culture and history, but is also inclusive of other writers of color, including Native American, European, Asian, and Latinx authors. These books were meant to provide her with a strong sense of her identity beyond the dominant cultural take on history that she receives as a student in a predominantly white, Southern public school system. This library assumed new significance when we decided to share it with other students in her elementary school classroom.

During our daughter's first through third-grade elementary school experience, my husband and I volunteered as classroom readers. We took this responsibility very seriously and would choose the two to three books that we would read in class the night before. Favorite choices included *Elena's Serenade* by Campbell Geeslin, *A Boy and a Jaguar* (2014) by Alan Rabionowitz, and *The Other Side* (2001) by Jacqueline Woodson. I recall one day in particular when I decided to read Japanese American author Allen Say's *Grandfather's Journey* (1993). The book is both a transgenerational reverse migration and immigration tale. I was only a few pages into the story when an Asian student in the class excitedly raised his hand. When I paused and asked if he had a question, he pointed to the page I was reading and said, "That's like me. That's my grandfather." I went on to ask if he took trips to visit his grandfather sometimes, and he nodded his head enthusiastically before I picked up the story again. As much as conservatives have made identity politics a nasty word, the desire to see oneself in the stories we share begins at an early age. While this student experienced a deeply personal reaction to an Asian protagonist, his non-Asian peers could relate to the story as well through the narrative trope of visiting grandparents.

My husband and I stepped into the gap in our daughter's classroom because we were not afraid to introduce discussions of race and cultural difference to kids, and we hoped doing so would make her school a safer place for her and other students of color who otherwise would not hear or see stories representative of their lives. While doing so, we would occasionally glance over our shoulders to see if her teacher was listening in, particularly when we read books like *Separate is Never Equal: Sylvia Mendez & Her Family's Fight for Desegregation* (2014), a story about a Mexican-American family that fought to win the right for their daughter, an American citizen, to attend a white school in 1944. The story is based on the legal case that predated and set the groundwork for Brown v. Board of Education. The book begins after the three-year battle for their daughter to integrate the local white school has been won. What their daughter then experiences explains why integration is only the beginning of the race re-education project. On the first day in the new school wearing her "shiny-new" black shoes, "a young white boy pointed at her and yelled, 'Go back to the Mexican school! You don't belong here!'" Despite its frankness, the book has a happy ending. The remainder of the story discusses in detail how Sylvia gains the strength to find real friends at her new school.

Some educators still balk at the idea of using a book that discusses race using clear terminology of white, black, or Japanese, but these are terms that students encounter on a regular basis in the conversations of their parents, television shows, social media, and on the playground. If they are not given a healthy context for these terms, they will just buy into whichever source speaks most loudly in their lives. If the source is a biased one, the students will eventually act out on this racial bias in aggressive and socially destructive ways among their peers.

When my husband read *Separate is Never Equal* in our daughter's class, he had to contend with pronouncing the Spanish words that pepper the text. He chose French as his second language for his formal education, so his Spanish accent was a little questionable. One of the shyest girls in class, a Mexican American student, suddenly stepped in to correct his pronunciation as he continued to read. My husband and her peers were duly impressed and pleased with her contribution to storytime that day.

If asked, teachers will often say that they don't read books that discuss race because they are uncomfortable doing so. With so many Coretta Scott King, Caldecott, and Pura Belpre award-winning children's books to choose from, there is no reason not to feel empowered enough to dig in. It is key that early childhood educators take a central role in teaching racial tolerance in our schools to make them the truly integrated spaces that they should be.

While a lot of attention was paid to our daughter's diversity training, I realized that the same attention was not being shared with our younger, white son. His reading material largely consisted of young adult fantasy novels that he consumed at a rapid rate. While I was glad he was an avid reader, it bothered me that he knew very little about African American culture or history and could not relate at all to his sister's social condition as a black girl. Nor would he understand what would be in store for her as a POC in the future. Our younger daughter, in effect, was bearing the racial burden of her social oppression while statistics showed her brother would actually one day be in a position of power that would have a greater impact on the lives of people of color. In other words, privilege would give him power over POC but no intellectual foundation for understanding these communities.

Despite having a black sister, at this rate he would likely remain a cultural and racial outsider to her world.

There is only one remedy for racial alienation, and that is racial inclusion, but many wonder how this can be accomplished amid the current free speech/hate speech divide in America. The clamor of white nationalism has dangerously occluded a very real history of proactive racial alliances at work in America for generations. Sadly, a distilled, prejudicial version of history has all but erased these alliances that deconstruct the notion of a racist white monolith. The type of historical alliances of which I speak took place as recently as the pre-Civil War era surrounding the issue of American slavery.

One of the elements of American slavery neglected by films about the institution is that black-authored slave narratives were prefaced by an authenticating statement penned by a white person of character. These authenticating statements served to renounce the myths that Africans were incapable of literacy by vouching for the black-authored narrative a white reader was preparing to consume. For example, while recently teaching Harriet Jacobs's *Incidents in the Life of a Slave Girl* (1861), I drew student attention to Lydia Maria Child's introduction, where she deconstructs prevailing denial of African intellectual capacity. She pointedly praises Jacobs's literary merit to redefine black and white female empowerment in the nineteenth century. On the one hand, she defends Jacobs's intellect and her right not to be victimized by a sexual exploitation that was the result of enslavement. Conversely, she calls on a white literate female audience to empower themselves by reading and surely empathizing with a black woman's story of sexual and racial oppression. In the end, my students understood that interracial "ally" relationships took place in the nineteenth century in the same way they took place during multiracial die-ins over protests surrounding the deaths of Eric Garner and Michael Brown in 2014. When studying American literary history, there is no need for white guilt and black victimization to stand as uncomplicated roles students must still play in the twenty-first century. Stated another way, white students don't need to assume the guilt-ridden role of slaver, and black students don't need to accept the impotent role of victimized slave. The importance of studying slave history is to understand how the lack of knowledge about these historical relationships still undermines racial progress. If the truth is examined through a transhistorical lens, there is plenty of room to celebrate a transracial American radical tradition tied to social progress.

Finally, an essential aspect of any radical tradition is coming to consciousness. Consciousness-raising is the process by which new knowledge becomes a gateway to understanding. Consider the #MeToo movement and its outing of known perpetrators of inappropriate sexual harassment as a case in point. The movement, founded by African American activist Tarana Burke, was fully endorsed by white women eager to tell their stories of sexual exploitation. Now the general public, through consciousness-raising, is much more aware of what constitutes sexual harassment and unacceptable behavior, regardless of one's racial, economic, or educational background. Clearly, as a nation, we must arm both our sons and daughters of all races with each other's stories to see social progress of any kind.

REFERENCES

Chapter I:

Brokeback Mountain. Dir. Ang Lee, Performances by Heath Ledger, Jake Gyllenhaal, and Michelle Williams, Focus Features, 2005.

Douglass, Frederick. *The Narrative of the Life of Frederick Douglass, an American Slave. 1845.* W.W. Norton, 2016.

Gonzalez, Rigoberto. *Red-Inked Retablos.* The University of Arizona Press, 2013.

Kahf, Mohja. *The Girl in the Tangerine Scarf.* Carroll & Graf Publishers, 2006.

Chapter 2:

Draper, Sharon M. *Blended.* Atheneum, 2019.

Durrow, Heidi. *The Girl Who Fell From the Sky.* Algonquin, 2010.

Hairston, Peter. W. *The Cooleemee Plantation and Its People.* Hunter Publishing Company, 1986.

Loving. Dir. Jeff Nichols, performances by Joel Edgerton and Ruth Negga, Focus Features, 2016.

McBride, James. *The Color of Water: A Black Man's Tribute to His White Mother.* Penguin, 1995.

Senna, Danzy. *Where Did You Sleep Last Night? A Personal History.* Farrar, Straus, and Giroux, 2009.

Trethewey, Natasha. *Native Guard.* Mariner Books, 2007.

Chapter 3:

Coates, Ta-Nehisi. *Between the World and Me*. Spiegel & Grau, 2015.

Wiesel, Elie. *Night*. 1958. Farrar, Straus, Giroux, 2006.

Chapter 4:

Cullen, Countee. *The Black Christ and Other Poems*. Harper, 1929. Also see: Countee Cullen: Collected Poems. Ed. Major Jackson. Library of America, 2013.

Night and Fog. Dir. Alain Resnais, Argos Films, 1956.

Wells-Barnett, Ida B. *The Red Record: Tabulated Statistics and Alleged Causes of Lynching in the United States*. 1895. Cavalier Classics, 2015.

"Without Sanctuary: Lynching Photography in America."withoutsanctuary.org.

Chapter 5:

Introducing Dorothy Dandridge. Dir. Martha Coolidge, performances by Halle Berry, Home Box Office, 1999.

Chapter 6:

Daughters of the Dust. Dir. Julie Dash, performances by Barbara O. and Alva Rogers, Kino International, 1991.

Long Soldier, Layli. *Whereas*. Graywolf, 2017.

Silko, Leslie Marmon. *Ceremony*. 1977. Penguin, 2006.

Smoke Signals. Dir. Chris Eyre, performances by Adam Beach and Irene Bedard. Miramax, 1998.

Text-S.J. Res. 14—111th Congress (2009-2010) Congressional Apology to the Native American People.

Chapter 7:

12 Years a Slave. Dir. Steve McQueen, performances by Chiwetel Ejiofor, Lupita Nyong'o, and Brad Pitt, Fox Searchlight Pictures, 2013.

Black Girl. Dir. Ousmane Scmbène, performance by Mbissine Thérèse Diop, New Yorker Video, 1966.

Bulawayo, NoViolet: *We Need New Names.* Back Bay Books, 2014.

El Saadawi, Nawal. *Woman at Point Zero.* Zed Books, 1983.

Joseph Conrad. *Heart of Darkness.* 1902. W.W. Norton, 2005.

Moolaadé. Dir. Ousmane Sembène, performance by Fatoumata Coulibaly, 2004.

Ngozi Adichie, Chimamanda. *Americanah.* Random House, 2013.

Walker, Alice. *Possessing the Secret of Joy.* Washington Square Press, 1992.

Chapter 8:

Alexie, Sherman. *You Don't Have to Say you Love Me.* Little, Brown and Company, 2017.

Erdrich, Louise. *LaRose.* HarperCollins, 2016.

Chapter 9:

Komunyakaa, Yusef. *Dien Cai Dau*. Wesleyan UP, 1988.

Morrison, Toni. *Sula*.1973. Plume, 1982.

Vuong, Ocean. *Night Sky With Exit Wounds*. Copper Canyon P, 2016.

Chapter 11:

Du Bois, WEB. *The Souls of Black Folk*. 1903. Bedford Books,1997.

Eady, Cornelius. *Brutal Imagination*. Penguin, 2001.

Hughes, Langston. *The Big Sea*. 1940. Farrar, Straus, Giroux, 1993.

James Baldwin's *The Fire Next Time*. 1962. Vintage International, 1993.

Pierce-Baker, Charlotte. *This Fragile Life: A Mother's Story of a Bipolar Son*. Lawrence Hill Books, 2012.

Southgate, Martha. *The Fall of Rome*. Scribner, 2002.

Walker, Frank X. *Turn Me Loose: The Unghosting of Medgar Evers*.The University of Georgia Press, 2013.

Chapter 13:

Alexander, Michelle. *The New Jim Crow*. The New Press, 2012.

Geeslin, Campbell. *Elena's Serenade*. Atheneum, 2004.

Rabinowitz, Alan. *A Boy and a Jaguar*. Houghton Mifflin, 2014.

Say, Allen. *Grandfather's Journey*. Houghton Mifflin, 1993.

Tonatiuh, Duncan. *Separate is Never Equal: Sylvia Mendez & Her Family's Fight for Desegregation.* Abrams Books, 2014.

Woodson, Jacqueline. *The Other Side.* G.P. Putnam's Sons, 2001.

Acknowledgements

The author wishes to thank the following publications for publishing versions of these chapters:

"A Lynching in North Carolina." Tupelo Quarterly, Winter 2018. Tupeloquarterly.com.
"Sonny Boy." The Hopkins Review 10.4 (A publication of Johns Hopkins University Press) Spring 2017.
"Pull and Drag." Blood Orange Review, Spring 2017. Bloodorangereview.com.

The author would also like to acknowledge the following organizations which provided valuable time and funding for this book: The Hambidge Center for Creative Arts and Sciences, the Mary Hambidge Fellowship, and the Appalachian College Association Faculty Fellowship.

SPECIAL THANKS

Special thanks are due to the following people who supported the writing of these essays in various ways: David Yezzi, Sharon Harrigan, Bridgett Davis, Evie Shockley, Deborah Norkin, and Gordon H. Bell. I would also like to thank New Rivers Press for giving this book a home. The pedagogical impetus for this collection took root many years ago when I worked with Deborah Mutnick at Long Island University and as an antiracism consultant in the New York City Public School System. These early-career experiences solidified for me the need for and efficacy of fighting racial and cultural bias through social justice literacy.

ABOUT THE AUTHOR

Artress Bethany White PhD is a poet, essayist, and literary critic. She is the recipient of the 2018 Trio Award for her poetry collection, *My Afmerica* (Trio House Press, 2019). *Survivor's Guilt: Essays on Race and American Identity* is her first essay collection. She is also the author of the poetry collection *Fast Fat Girls In Pink Hot Pants* (2012). Her prose and poetry have appeared in such journals as *Harvard Review*, *Tupelo Quarterly*, *The Hopkins Review*, *Pleiades, Solstice, Poet Lore*, *Ecotone*, and *The Account*. Scholarly essays appear in the anthologies *Seeking Home: Marginalization and Representation in Appalachian Letters and Song* (U of Tennessee P, 2017) and *Literary Expressions of African Spirituality* (Lexington Books, 2013). White has received the Mary Hambidge Distinguished Fellowship from the Hambidge Center for Creative Arts for her nonfiction, The Mona Van Duyn Scholarship in Poetry from the Sewanee Writers' Conference, and writing residencies at The Writer's Hotel and the Tupelo Press/MASS MoCA studios. She teaches poetry and nonfiction workshops for Rosemont College in Philadelphia. (Author Website: Artressbethanywhite. com)

ABOUT NEW RIVERS PRESS

New Rivers Press emerged from a drafty Massachusetts barn in winter 1968. Intent on publishing work by new and emerging poets, founder C.W. "Bill" Truesdale labored for weeks over an old Chandler & Price letterpress to publish three hundred fifty copies of Margaret Randall's collection *So Many Rooms Has a House but One Roof.* About four hundred titles later, New Rivers is now a nonprofit learning press, based since 2001 at Minnesota State University Moorhead. Charles Baxter, one of the first authors with New Rivers, calls the press "the hidden backbone of the American literary tradition."

As a learning press, New Rivers guides student editors, designers, writers, and filmmakers through the various processes involved in selecting, editing, designing, publishing, and distributing literary books. In working, learning, and interning with New Rivers Press, students gain integral real-world knowledge that they bring with them into the publishing workforce at positions with publishers across the country, or to begin their own small presses and literary magazines.

Please visit our website: newriverspress.com for more information.